INDIA'S CHINA POLICY

P. C. Chakravarti

INDIA'S CHINA POLICY

INDIANA UNIVERSITY PRESS

Bloomington 1962

CONTENTS

MAPS

PREFACE

THIS SHORT survey of recent India-China relations has been written more for the general reader than for the select band of scholars and administrators. I have, therefore, deliberately refrained from burdening the book with too many details and footnotes, and have attempted to state the essential facts and the conclusions emerging from them within as short a compass as possible.

"The key to Sino-Indian relations lies hidden in the soil of Tibet. It is on the rocks of the Roof of the World that our friendship with China will flourish or founder." This is what I stated some years ago in the course of a Jadavpur University Extension Lecture. Strangely enough, this obvious proposition was then greeted with derision in certain political and intellectual circles in Calcutta. Subsequent events have, however, confirmed the validity of this view. Tibet may or may not be the "roof of the world," but it is certainly the roof of India. Any strong expansionist power, entrenched in Tibet, holds in its hands a loaded pistol pointed at the heart of

India. Tibetan developments, therefore, find a prominent place in the story which I have recounted. In fact, the title of the book might well have been "Tibet in India-China Relations."

This survey may be considered controversial on the grounds of its subject matter. It will be no less controversial on account of the readiness with which I have called a spade a spade, when necessary. I frankly confess that I have looked at the whole problem of our relations with China from the standpoint of an Indian who loves his country, its freedom and its democratic way of life. I do not deny that there may be other points of view different from mine.

A major part of the book was written while I was in the United States for a few months in 1960, working at Indiana University, Bloomington, and the University of California, Berkeley. I am thankful to the library staffs of these universities, in particular to Mr. Cecil Byrd, Associate Director of the Indiana University Library, for their ungrudging assistance while I was working on the book. I am also grateful to Professor Walter H. C. Laves, Chairman, Department of Government, Indiana University, and to Mrs. Margaret Fisher of the University of California for their friendly interest. Above all, I am indebted to Professor Joseph L. Sutton, Chairman, Asian Studies Program, Indiana University, for his encouragement and helpful comments, and for facilitating the publication of the book by the Indiana University Press.

My deep appreciation is also due to some of my Indian friends with whom I discussed my views on India-China relations.

P. C. CHAKRAVARTI

Jadavpur University, Calcutta
March 30, 1961

INDIA'S CHINA POLICY

chapter 1

HISTORIC FRIENDSHIP

FOR ALMOST a decade few slogans were more popular or more uncritically accepted in India than that which described the Indians and the Chinese as brothers—*Hindi Chini Bhai Bhai*. It was more than a mere slogan; constant reiteration had almost turned it into an article of national faith. Leaders, platform speakers, and columnists all swore by the "age-old," "historic," and "eternal" friendship between India and China; and anyone who questioned the validity of this concept of friendship ran the risk of being insulted and abused. Chinese leaders and politicians have also used the same slogans, but always in a Pickwickian sense. Premier Chou En-lai of China has never tired of reminding India of the "eternal friendship between our two countries," while he converted Tibet into a base of operations, shot down and imprisoned Indian frontier guards on Indian soil, and forcibly intruded into and occupied Indian territory.

It is, therefore, of some interest to examine the history and rationale of this concept of friendship between India and

China. The history of India's relations with China indeed goes back to the distant past. When Buddhism spread to China in the early centuries of the Christian era, naturally a kind of spiritual kinship grew up between the land which gave birth to the Buddha and his votaries in other lands. From about the third century, Chinese monks began to visit India to pay homage to the places sanctified by the memory of the Buddha, collect authentic Buddhist manuscripts, and drink deep in the fountain of Indian learning. The most noteworthy among these Chinese pilgrims were Fa-hien (Indian visit 399-414 A.D.), Yuan Chwang (30-643 A.D.), and I-tsing (671-695 A.D.). Many Indian scholars too went to China and dedicated their lives to the pious task of translating Buddhist texts into the Chinese language. The most famous among them were Dharmaraksha (middle of the third century), Kumarajiva (401 A.D.), Gunavarma (431 A.D.), and Dharmagupta (590 A.D.).

The relationship which was thus built up by monks and scholars between India and China was essentially a spiritual and cultural relationship. It was, moreover, largely a one-way traffic. India gave: China received. Indian thought deeply tinged Chinese civilization; but India received hardly anything in return. There is no evidence of Chinese thought influencing Indian civilization, unless it be that some latter-day Hindu dynasties derived vicariously some of their notions regarding the divinity that "doth hedge a king" from Chinese sources.

With the conquest of India by Islamic invaders from the northwest, and the virtual disappearance of Buddhism from Indian soil, the old spiritual and cultural links between India and China were, however, snapped. And throughout the centuries when the Turko-Afghans and the Mughals ruled over India, the relations between the two countries amounted to very little beyond the dispatch of one or two missions of small consequence and a slight, intermittent trickle of trade by sea.

A new kind of relations, however, grew up between the two countries early in the twenties of this century. The impact of the West had led to a tremendous intellectual renaissance in India in the nineteenth century; and this was followed, as in Europe, by a religious and spiritual revival and a new demand for political freedom. The Indian National Congress was founded in 1885, but the real struggle for freedom commenced with the anti-partition (of Bengal) and Swadeshi movement in 1905. It was the year when Japan won her spectacular victory over Russia, and this smashing success which the "dwarf of the East" won over "the colossus of the West" had an immediate, electrifying effect on Indian minds. In fact, from this date Japan cast a spell over the Indian intelligentsia which lasted well over two decades. It was only when Japan turned on her career of aggression against China that the spell began to wear out, and India's great poet, Rabindranath Tagore, wrote with deep sorrow: "I can no longer point out with pride the example of a great Japan."

After centuries of comparative aloofness and isolation, the sympathies of India were drawn toward China by the spectacle of her sufferings and her heroic struggle against tremendous odds. India herself was fighting against British imperialism. China was striving hard to maintain her political entity against a whole series of imperialist powers, Western and Eastern. Out of this common struggle against imperialism emerged new ties of friendship, new sympathies, a new desire to help each other and learn from each other. China watched with great interest Mahatma Gandhi's non-cooperation and civil disobedience movement of 1920-21, and her great leader, Dr. Sun Yat-sen, in his lecture on the methods of nationalism, which was later incorporated in his "Three People's Principles," pointed to the Indian movement as an object lesson for the Chinese nationalists.[1] In India, the All-India Congress Committee, meeting at Patna in 1925, expressed its deep sympathy with the Chinese "in their struggle against the alien domination of their land," and further recorded "its most emphatic

protest against the dispatch of the Indian soldiers by the
Government of India to suppress the Chinese national movement of freedom." Again, in December, 1927, the Indian
National Congress, meeting at Madras, sent its warmest greetings to the people of China and its assurance of full sympathy
with them "in their fight for emancipation."[2] The Congress
also recorded its demand that all Indian troops and police
forces be recalled forthwith and that no Indian should go to
China in future "as an agent of the British Government to
fight or work against the Chinese people, who, in the opinion
of the Congress, are the comrades of the Indian people in
their joint struggle against imperialism."

India's sympathies and interest in the struggle and fortunes
of China became even more pronounced in the thirties. Between 1931 and 1933 Japan seized Manchuria, besieged and
partly burned Shanghai, and invaded Jehol, north of Peking.
In 1935 she attempted to seize another large section of northern
China and actually occupied northern Chahar and eastern
Hopei. Commenting on these events, Pandit Jawaharlal Nehru,
presiding over the Indian National Congress meeting at
Lucknow in 1936, said:

In the Far East also war hovers on the horizon, and we see an
eastern imperialism advancing methodically and pitilessly over
ancient China and dreaming of world empire. . . . Imperialism
shows its claws wherever it may be, in the West or in the East. . . .
To the progressive forces in the world, to those who stand for
human freedom and the breaking of political and social bonds, we
offer our full cooperation in their struggle against imperialism
and fascist reaction, for we realise that our struggle is a common
one.[3]

Other Indian leaders made similar statements condemning
Japanese imperialism and expressing sympathy with China
in her heroic struggle. Yone Noguchi, the well-known Japanese
poet, dismayed by the reaction produced on the Indian mind
by what Japan was doing in China, wrote a letter to Tagore

attempting to justify Japanese action and advocating the
doctrine of "Asia for Asians." "Believe me," he wrote, "it is a
war of 'Asia for Asia'. With a crusader's determination and
with a sense of sacrifice that belongs to a martyr, our young
soldiers go to the front. Their minds are light and happy,
because the war is not for conquest, but the correction of
the mistaken idea of China, . . . and for uplifting her simple
but ignorant masses to better life and wisdom." To this Tagore
replied that "no amount of special pleading can change the
fact that in launching a ravening war on Chinese humanity,
with all the deadly methods learnt from the West, Japan is
infringing on every moral principle on which civilization is
based. . . . You are building your conception of an Asia which
would be raised on a tower of skulls."[4]

In 1937 and 1938 the Indian National Congress again
passed resolutions expressing its sympathy with the Chinese
in their struggle against a "ruthless and inhuman imperialism"
and congratulating them on their heroic resistance. It organized a number of China Days in India, in which demonstrations were held all over the country and funds were collected
with a view to offering financial assistance to the Chinese in
their hour of distress. It also organized a boycott of Japanese
goods in India, which brought about a sharp decline in Indo-
Japanese trade. Finally, it sent an ambulance corps to China
under the leadership of Dr. M. Atal, who had previously seen
service in the Spanish Civil War, as a gesture of India's good
will and of "India's solidarity with China."

In August, 1939, Pandit Jawaharlal Nehru himself went on
a good-will mission to China with the blessings of Mahatma
Gandhi and Rabindranath Tagore, "to convey the affection
and sympathy of the people of India to the Chinese people,"
and "bring back something of the courage and invincible
optimism of the Chinese people and their capacity to pull
together when peril confronts them." He was warmly received
by the people and leaders of China including Generalissimo

and Madame Chiang Kai-shek. In an address to the Chinese
people, broadcast by the Chungking radio (August 30, 1939),
Nehru stressed the importance of Sino-Indian cooperation "for
the sake of the freedom of our dearly-loved countries, for Asia
and for the world," and he returned from China with a love
for that country excelled, to quote Mahatma Gandhi, if at all,
only by his love of his own country.[5]

In 1940 China, on her part, sent two missions to India—one
a good-will mission led by Tai Chi-tao and the other a cultural
mission headed by Dr. K. Wellington Koo of the Chinese
Ministry of Education. In 1942 Generalissimo Chiang Kai-shek
came on a visit to India primarily to discuss political and military matters with the British authorities, but he took advantage
of the opportunity to meet Gandhi, Nehru, and other Indian
leaders. In the public statement issued at the time of his visit,
he expressed the hope that Great Britain, "without waiting for
any demands on the part of the people of India, will as
speedily as possible, give them their political powers."

In August, 1942, Mahatma Gandhi decided to initiate what
has become known as the "Quit India" movement as a last
desperate measure to force the British to concede independence to India. The war was at a critical stage. In the Far
East, Britain, China, and the United States were fighting
jointly against Japan. It was clear that a civil disobedience
movement in India at that crucial hour might be widely mis-
understood; it might be construed as a movement designed
to sabotage the war effort. But Gandhi was anxious that at least
Generalissimo Chiang Kai-shek should not misunderstand him.
Before taking the final decision, therefore, he wrote a long
letter to the Generalissimo, explaining his point of view. "Because of the feeling I have toward China," he wrote, "I am
anxious to explain to you that my appeal to the British power
to withdraw from India is not meant in any shape or form to
weaken India's defence against the Japanese or to embarrass
you in your struggle. . . . I would not be guilty of purchasing

the freedom of my country at the cost of your country's free-dom. . . . Whatever action I may recommend will be governed by the consideration that it should not injure China or en-courage Japanese aggression in India or China."[6]

In 1944 Dr. S. Radhakrishnan, who had built up a world-wide reputation as an interpreter of Eastern thought, went on a lecture tour to China and spoke eloquently on the "common cultural and spiritual background" and the "similar ideals of human life and fellowship" in the civilizations of India and China.[7]

Those were the days of Sino-Indian honeymoon, when two of the greatest countries of Asia, each inheritor of a great past, marched hand in hand to shake off foreign domination and build a "brave new world" on the basis of freedom and democracy. In fact, some Indian leaders even thought and spoke in terms of an "Asiatic Federation." In 1930 an attempt was made to summon a meeting of what was called a Pan-Asiatic Federation in India. Nehru himself, on his first visit to China in 1939, spoke of his vision of the future when there would be a federation of Asian states including China, India, Burma, Ceylon, Afghanistan, and "possibly other countries." In the light of experience, all this talk of Asian federation would appear to have been nothing more than an idle dream. But Indian leaders had not yet been invested with the responsibility of guiding the destinies of their country, and they could afford to indulge in dreams.

The dreams were not, however, destined to last for long. With the termination of the Second World War a new land-scape emerged in Asia. The victory of the Allies meant the victory of China. She had already been accepted as a major power, at least by the United States, at the Cairo Conference of 1943, where it was promised that all the territories pre-viously taken from her by Japan would be restored. For India, too, victory was in sight in her struggle for independence. Great Britain was exhausted by the war and perturbed by the

mounting tensions in India. The Labor Party, which had come
into power in 1945, decided to hand over the Indian government to the Indians, and in August 1957 India took her place
among the fully self-governing nations. Other Asian countries
were also on the march, and some of them, such as Burma
and Indonesia, had many cultural ties with India. Under these
new conditions relations between India and China could not
remain unaffected.

The first symptom of this change appeared in March, 1947,
when an unofficial Inter-Asia Relations Conference was held
at New Delhi under the auspices of the Indian Council of
World Affairs. The purpose of the conference was to review
the position of Asia in the postwar world, exchange ideas on
problems common to all Asian countries, and study ways and
means of promoting closer contacts between them. The conference was attended by delegates from China, the Philippines,
Indonesia, Indochina, Malaya, Burma, Ceylon, Thailand, five
Asian republics of the U.S.S.R., Egypt, Palestine, and other
countries. Of all the delegations at the conference the tactics
pursued by those from China were, according to observers, by
far the most interesting and involved.[8] They did not quite
relish the presence of the Tibetan delegates at the conference,
but as the latter scarcely participated in the discussions, the
Chinese refrained from making any open comments about it.
They did object, however, to a map of Asia displayed in the
conference hall in which Tibet was shown as a political entity
separate from China. Ultimately George Yeh, who was then
the Director of the European Affairs Department of the
Ministry of Foreign Affairs in China and who attended the
Conference as an observer, protested about it to Nehru and
the map was removed.[9] What was worrying the Chinese delegates more than anything else, however, was that India might
"run away with the leadership of the Conference," and they
conducted a relentless backstage campaign to forestall any
such eventuality. There was a proposal before the Conference

of a permanent Asian organization, and it was in regard to the character and locale of this organization "that the leaders of Asia's two greatest nations locked horns."[10] The Chinese did not wish to be tied to an organization in which India played the leader's role. Nor did India relish the idea of surrendering the leadership to China. There was a rift in the lute of Sino-Indian solidarity. In the world of nation-states national interests are bound, in the ultimate analysis, to dominate national policies. India, like China, had at last become a nation, and slowly but inexorably this fact asserted itself in Indian and Chinese thinking in international affairs.

During the next two years (1947-49) cordial relations between India and China visibly waned. On formal occasions, when diplomats presented their credentials and in public meetings, the leaders of both the countries still spoke in terms of "long-standing" Sino-Indian friendship and cultural affinities, but Indian press comments became openly critical of China's internal and external policies. In knowledgeable circles there were guarded comments on the "corruption," "nepotism," and "tyranny" of the Chiang Kai-shek regime and its dependence on the Western powers, althought there were no friendly comments, except in Communist circles, on the advancing tide of Communism.

In January, 1949, the Indian government called an official Asian conference at Delhi to consider the renewed military operations of the Netherlands government against Indonesia. Speaking at Allahabad on January 1, 1949, Prime Minister Nehru said that the Dutch had committed an act of "naked and unabashed aggression" in their attempt "to revive a dying imperialism which India and, he believed, other countries of Asia could not tolerate." India and Pakistan informed the Netherlands government that they would not permit the Royal Dutch Airlines (K.L.M.) to land or cross the territories of their countries. The government of Ceylon announced that Dutch ships or aircraft carrying troops, arms, or warlike material of any kind which might be used against the Indonesian people would be denied access to any Ceylonese port or air field. The Delhi Conference, which met from January 20 to 23, was attended by delegates from eighteen countries. But China was represented only by observers, and all through the crisis she followed what may be described as a sitting-on-the-fence policy. This may have been due to the fact that she was preoccupied with her own civil war, in which the Communists were unmistakably getting the upper hand. It may have been due to the influence of the wealthy Chinese community in Indonesia, which had clearly more sympathies with the Dutch imperialists than with the Indonesian nationalists. But it may as well have been due to her dislike of the preponderant role which India was playing in this conference as she did in the Inter-Asian Conference of 1947.[11]

chapter 2

TIBET AND ITS HISTORICAL STATUS

THE CIVIL war between the Kuomintang and the Communists in China was practically over by September, 1949, and on October 1 the Communists proclaimed the formal inauguration of the People's Republic of China with Mao Tse-tung at the head and Chou En-lai as premier and foreign Minister. The Chinese Communists had nothing but contempt for independent India, its government and its leaders. For months their press had indulged in wild attacks on independent India as "an agent of Western imperialism." Replying to a message of greetings from the Indian Communist party, Mao Tse-tung stated on October 19, 1949:

I firmly believe that relying on the brave Communist Party of India and the unity and struggle of all Indian patriots, India will certainly not remain long under the yoke of imperialism and its collaborators. Like free China, free India will one day emerge in the socialist and People's Democratic family; that day will end the imperialist reactionary era in the history of mankind.[1]

In other words, free India still needed to be "liberated" through the establishment of a Communist regime. It was clear that to the Communists, the achievement of political power on the mainland of China was merely the beginning, not the culmination, of their revolution, and Mao's statement darkly hinted at their ambitious international goals.

But unperturbed either by the character of the Chinese revolution or by its half-expressed ambitions, the government of India was anxious from the beginning to befriend Mao's China. In fact, India was the second non-Communist country in the world to accord diplomatic recognition to the new regime.[2] Explaining the Indian government's stand, Prime Minister Nehru stated: "It was not a question of approving or disapproving the changes that have taken place. It was a question of recognising a major event in history and appreciating and dealing with it. The new Government is a stable government and there is no force likely to supplant it or push it away." In presenting his credentials to Mao Tse-tung, Chairman of the People's Republic of China, the Indian ambassador, Sardar K. M. Panikkar, went far beyond the usual diplomatic politeness and said: "The People's Republic of China and the Republic of India, representing the oldest communities in the world, are now in a position to cooperate effectively for mutual advantage and for the welfare of their people. The two sister republics of Asia, which between them contain over a third of the world's population, can through their cooperation become a great and invincible force."[3] Some time later, when the first Ambassador of Communist China, General Yuan Chung-shien, arrived at the Delhi railway station, he was received with an ovation the like of which was seldom accorded to foreign ambassadors arriving at the capital.

But a new difficulty, to which India could not be indifferent, soon cropped up. On January 1, 1950 (only two days after Indian recognition) the new regime in China proclaimed that one of the basic tasks of the "People's Liberation Army" would henceforth be to "liberate" Tibet and "stand guard at the Chinese frontiers." On August 5, the New China News

Agency quoted General Liu Po-chen, Chairman of the South-west China Military Affairs Commission, as stating that Tibet must be brought back to the "Motherland's big family" and "China's defence line must be consolidated." On September 30, the first anniversary of the establishment of the People's Republic of China, Chou En-lai reiterated his Government's determination to "liberate" Tibet from "imperialist aggression." It was clear that the Communists were planning the subjugation of Tibet as a part of their program to reconquer those territories along the periphery of China which had once belonged to the Chinese empire or paid allegiance to the Dragon Throne.

A great deal has been written in recent years about the historical status of Tibet. Some have contended that Tibet had always been an integral part of China and had no legal or moral right to secede from the parent body and lead an independent life of its own. Others have maintained that whatever might have been the nature of relations between China and Tibet in the two centuries preceding 1912, the hermit kingdom had been for all practical purposes independent after that date, and that reconquest of Tibet by China could be justified only on the principle that might makes right. It is therefore necessary to state the main facts of the historical relationship between Tibet and China.

There was hardly any kind of political relationship between Tibet and China, apart from occasional marriages, and wars which the Tibetans sometimes won, until the great Mongol Kublai Khan, whose dominions extended over more than half of Asia and parts of Europe, was converted to Buddhism by some lamas from Tibet, the chief among them being Pak-pa of the Sakya monastery. Even as a prince Kublai had been so deeply impressed by the young nephew of the Sakya abbot and a few other lamas from Tibet that as soon as he became the great Khan, he asked Pak-pa to be his spiritual guide or mentor. Waddell tells a story of how Kublai Khan asked some

Christian missionaries and the Tibetan lamas to perform a miracle to satisfy and convince him of the truth of their respective doctrines. The missionaries were unable to comply with the Khan's demand, but the lamas caused his wine-cup to rise miraculously to his lips.[4] For twelve years Pak-pa remained with the Emperor, at whose request he framed for the Mongol language an alphabet imitated from the Tibetan, which, however, did not prove successful. In return for his services, Kublai invested Pak-pa with sovereign powers over (1) Tibet proper, comprising thirteen districts, (2) Southeastern Tibet (Kham), and (3) Amdo, a province in northeastern Tibet.

The relations which were thus formed between Tibet and the Mongol emperors were essentially like those between a layman and his priest. They were not the relations between a conqueror and the conquered or between an overlord and his vassal. As a result of the arrangements made in the time of Kublai Khan, the Grand Lamas of the Sakya monastery in Tibet became the spiritual mentors and consecrators of the Tuan emperors. In return the emperors were expected to guarantee Tibet's protection.

These relations, however, did not survive the fall of the Tuan dynasty (1368), and during the next three centuries, when the Ming emperors ruled over China (1368-1644), there is no evidence of any kind of spiritual or political relations being maintained between Tibet and China. These centuries witnessed the rise of the Yellow Hats sect and the emergence of the institution of the Dalai Lama in Tibet. When the Fifth Dalai Lama (usually called the Great Fifth) went on a visit to Peking at the invitation of the Chinese emperor, he was received with all the ceremony usually accorded a great, independent sovereign, and, as Rockhill says, "nothing can be found in any Chinese works to indicate that he was looked upon in any other light."[5]

In fact, Tibet continued to be an independent country outside the orbit of the Chinese empire until the first quarter of the eighteenth century. In 1717 a Mongol tribe from Turkestan called Dzungars swept down into Tibet and took Lhasa by storm, wrecking and looting monasteries and temples including the great Potala. In their distress the Tibetans appealed to the Chinese emperor, K'ang-hsi, for help against the marauders. For nearly seventy years (1690-1738), the foreign policy of the Chinese emperors was dominated by a tenacious struggle with these Dzungars. At last the emperor found an opportunity of dealing them a crushing blow. In 1720 he sent three armies which defeated the Dzungars in a series of skirmishes and battles and thus compelled them to withdraw from Tibet.[6]

The Chinese thus came into Tibet as deliverers. They did not, however, leave after the deliverance was complete, but continued as masters. This was the beginning of the Chinese protectorate over Tibet—a protectorate which continued for well-nigh two centuries. For the maintenance of the protectorate, the emperors installed two Ambans (Residents or Viceroys) and a Chinese expeditionary force at Lhasa. In the following two centuries, however, Chinese authority over Tibet waxed and waned with the changing fortunes of the central government at Peking. When that government was strong, their authority was real; when weak, it was nominal. The Tibetans, however, revolted against the Chinese when their yoke proved too galling or when opportunity was favorable. On such occasions, they expelled the Ambans, massacred the garrison, and threw off every semblance of Chinese overlordship. In fact, there is no evidence to suggest that the Chinese protectorate over Tibet was at any time based on the willing consent of the Tibetan people. It was tolerated so long as it operated from behind the veil; the moment it sought to supersede the Dalai Lama or impinge on his authority, it produced hostile reactions.

But whatever the character of Chinese authority over Tibet, it clearly began to crumble toward the end of the nineteenth century. China herself was decadent and disintegrating.

In 1895 she was disastrously defeated by Japan. In 1900 the Boxer Rebellion was routed by the Western armies. Taking advantage of this general political situation, the Thirteenth Dalai Lama so firmly reestablished his power as the spiritual and temporal ruler of Tibet that Chinese suzerainty was reduced to a mere pretense or, as Lord Curzon had put it, a mere "political affectation" and "a solemn farce."

This became more and more evident with every succeeding decade. In 1876 Great Britain had entered into a treaty with China whereby it was agreed, *inter alia,* that the Chinese government would make necessary arrangements for a British mission of exploration to visit Tibet. But no British mission could actually visit Tibet because the Tibetans refused to recognize the treaty or allow the mission to enter. Another Anglo-Chinese Convention was concluded in December, 1893, providing for the establishment of a trade mart at Yatung, eight miles on the Tibetan side of the Indo-Tibetan border. But the Tibetans again refused to recognize the treaty, and attempts to develop Yatung were frustrated by their obstructiveness.[7]

These repeated failures of the Chinese government to implement or enforce treaty provisions in respect of Tibetan territories brought home to the British government in India the full extent of Chinese impotence in Tibet. In was clear that if trade relations were to be opened up with Tibet or peace maintained on the Sikkim-Tibet frontier, the Indian government must negotiate with Lhasa rather than Peking. In 1899 Lord Curzon, then Viceroy of India, obtained the permission of His Majesty's Government in London to open direct negotiations with Tibet. Even then he found the Tibetans in no mood to negotiate; the Dalai Lama refused to receive the letters which Curzon arranged to be conveyed to him. Then came a further complicating factor. The Dalai Lama appeared to be carrying on negotiations with the Czar of Russia through one Djorieff, a Mongolian Buriat and Russian subject by birth, who journeyed to and fro between Lhasa and St.

Petersburg. Curzon could not afford to see Russian influence installed in Tibet; it would be too dangerous for Indian security. He decided to strike, and planned the expedition of 1904. The home government in London was reluctant to sanction the plan. They looked at the Tibetan question from the standpoint of an over-all imperial policy, while Curzon looked at it from the standpoint of Indian security. In the end he had his way. A limited expedition under Sir Francis Younghusband was sent into Tibet, which resulted in the Lhasa Convention of September, 1904. The Convention provided for the establishment of trade marts at Yatung, Gyantse, and Gartok, and the promotion and encouragement of commerce between India and Tibet. A British commercial agent was stationed at Gyantse, and was empowered to proceed, when necessity arose, to Lhasa. By Article 8 of the Convention the Tibetan government agreed to raze all forts and fortifications and remove all armaments which might impede the course of free navigation between the British frontier and the towns of Gyantse and Lhasa. Under Article 9 the government of Tibet undertook that without previous consent of the British Government

(a) No portion of Tibetan territory shall be ceded, sold, leased, mortgaged or otherwise given for occupation, to any foreign Power;

(b) No such Power shall be permitted to intervene in Tibetan affairs;

(c) No Representatives or Agents of any foreign Power shall be admitted to Thibet;

(d) No concessions for railways, roads, telegraphs, mining or other rights, shall be granted to any foreign Power, or the subject of any foreign Power. In the event of consent to such concessions being granted, similar or equivalent concessions shall be granted to the British Government.

(e) No Thibetan revenues, whether in kind or in cash, shall be pledged or assigned to any foreign Power, or to the subject of any foreign Power.

The Convention thus opened Tibet to British trade. It secured to Great Britain direct influence over the external policy of Tibet. It eliminated the danger of the Russian bear grimacing at India from the Roof of the World.

It is significant that throughout these transactions when a British army marched into Yatung and from Yatung to Lhasa and these drastic treaty provisions restricting national sovereignty were enforced on the Tibetans, there was not a word of protest from China. All that the Chinese Amban in Tibet did was to ingratiate himself with the British and then act as a go-between vis-à-vis the Tibetans on the one hand and the British on the other. In fact, as Sir Francis Younghusband admits, throughout the negotiations leading to the Convention the Amban was a great assistance to the British in enforcing their demands.[8] It is equally significant that the treaty was concluded between Great Britain and Tibet without reference to China. It bears the seals of the representatives of Tibet and those of the British government, but no seal of China. The conclusion of the treaty thus in a way proved that Tibet could act independently of China even in the matter of foreign policy.[9]

But once the threat from the north was removed and the main objectives of British policy secured, Britain felt no qualm of conscience in recognizing the fiction of Chinese suzerainty. So long as she had the substance, she felt no urge to chase the shadow. The shadow might, in fact, the British thought, be used to consolidate the gains. This seems to have been the *raison d'être* of British policy when Britain entered into a new convention with China in April, 1906, and another with Russia in August, 1907. Under the terms of the former, Britain not only secured a confirmation of her newly-acquired rights in Tibet but also the additional right to construct and maintain telegraph lines connecting Tibetan trade marts with India. Under the terms of the latter, Tibet was set up as a buffer zone between India and the Russian Asiatic empire.

Both Britain and Russia agreed to repect the integrity of Tibetan territory, abstain from any intervention in its internal administration, and treat with the government of Tibet only through its nominal suzerain, China. Britain, however, stipulated for herself the right of direct commerical relations with Tibet and obtained from Russia a recognition of her "special interest in the maintenance of *status quo* in the external relations of Tibet."

While ensuring the security of India by maintaining Tibet as a buffer zone, Britain at the same time was anxious to avoid doing anything which might seriously strain her relations with Russia. For she needed an understanding with Russia in the emerging contest for power in Europe. Germany under Kaiser Wilhelm II had posed a serious threat to British colonial interests and naval supremacy in the world. To meet this threat Britain had linked herself in an *Entente Cordiale* with France in 1904. Egged on by France, which had been an ally of Russia since 1894, and inspired by fear of Germany, which Russia and Britain equally shared, the two erstwhile adversaries decided to liquidate their outstanding differences in Asia by defining and delimiting their spheres of influence in areas of mutual conflict—Persia, Afghanistan, and Tibet. The resulting convention (1907) eminently fitted in with the British point of view. Tibet, like Afghanistan, became a protective cushion for India. The "farce" of Chinese suzerainty over Tibet was recognized (for the first time *expressis verbis* in the Anglo-Russian Convention) in the belief that it might serve as a thin outer cover for the cushion. In the circumstances of 1907 it would have required a prophet's vision to realize that the farce might one day become a reality, posing a more serious threat to Indian security than the Russian bear had ever done.

But one indirect result of the transactions of these years was that Tibet lay prostrate and China was technically left with a free hand to deal with that hapless country in any manner she liked. The Dalai Lama had been a fugitive since 1904. With the

mounting tension in Europe, The British Foreign Office became
preoccupied with European affairs. China found her opportunity and in 1910 again sent an invading army into Tibet, which
captured Lhasa, and pushing as far as Gartok and the border of
Ladakh, occupied the whole country. The Dalai Lama, who
had returned to Lhasa, after years of wandering, in December,
1909, again fled, this time to India. The Chinese deposed him.
Most Tibetans, however, mocked at the deposition and continued to regard the Dalai Lama as their lawful ruler. The out-
raged population of Lhasa tore down Chinese edicts and
proclamations or plastered them with dung.

But fortune again smiled on Tibet. In the autumn of 1911
there occurred the revolution in China leading to the fall of the
Manchu dynasty. The unrest spread to the Chinese garrisons in
Tibet. The troops mutinied, killed their officers, and moved
about looting the Tibetan people. Now the Tibetans rose in
insurrection against their oppressors, fought the Chinese garrisons, and eventually expelled them from their country. In June,
1912, the Dalai Lama returned from his exile, made a solemn
and pompous entrance at Lhasa, and assumed full and complete sovereign rights over the country. After years of struggle
and suffering, Tibet again became in fact an independent
country, though it was not recognized as such by other powers.
The Tibetans claimed that the old vassal-suzerain relationship,
which was based on the personal allegiance of the Dalai Lama
to the Manchu emperors, had come to an end with the extinc-
tion of the Manchu dynasty.

This did not mean that the new Chinese Republic accepted
the new de facto situation. It sought to ingratiate itself with the
Dalai Lama and induce him to recognize the suzerainty of
China over Tibet. Yuan Shi-kai, President of the new-born
Chinese Republic, telegraphed apologies for the excesses of
the Chinese troops and informed the Dalai Lama that his
original title and privileges would be restored. The Thirteenth
Dalai Lama, a politician and saint combined, replied that he

did not seek any title or privileges from the Chinese as he was the lawful religious and political ruler of an independent country.

When tension grew in the following months on account of Tibet's refusal to accept Chinese overlordship, the British, anxious for the maintenance of peace along India's northern frontier at a time when Europe appeared to be on the brink of a titanic world struggle, invited the Chinese and Tibetan representatives to a tripartite conference at Simla in the fall of 1913. The conference, which met in October, continued its sessions for six months and discussed very carefully the whole Tibetan question. But the viewpoints of the representatives appeared to be diametrically opposed. The Tibetans wanted nothing less than complete independence. The Chinese wanted the restoration of their protectorate over Tibet. The British were anxious to work out a compromise that would ensure security and peace along India's vital northern frontier.

In the end it was the British view which prevailed. Britain persuaded Tibet to recognize the nominal suzerainty of China. On April 27, 1914, a convention was initialed by the plenipotentiaries of the three governments. Under its terms Tibet was divided into two zones: (1) "Outer Tibet," skirting the Indian frontier and including Lhasa, Shigatse, and Chamdo, and (2) "Inner Tibet," contiguous to the Chinese frontier and comprising Ba-tong, Li-tang, Tachienlu, and a large portion of eastern Tibet. The suzerainty of China over both these zones was recognized. But China agreed to recognize the complete autonomy of "Outer Tibet" and to abstain from all interference in its administration. She engaged to abstain from sending troops, stationing civil or military officers, or establishing Chinese colonies there. In "Inner Tibet," however, China could send troops or officials and plant colonies; but the government of the Dalai Lama "were to retain their existing rights, which included, among other things, the control of most of the monasteries and the appointment of local chiefs."[10]

The Simla conference not only fixed the boundaries of Outer Tibet and set it up as a completely autonomous state having a nominal link with China; it also fixed the frontier between Tibet and northeastern India. The frontier from the east of Bhutan, along the northern and eastern border of Assam round to the meeting place of China, Tibet, and Burma—a distance of eight hundred and fifty miles—had never been clearly demarcated. In the years preceding the conference a large mass of data on geography, history, and custom had been carefully collected; these were now considered and the frontier between Tibet and India was fixed more or less along the ridges of the mountains, following the well-known watershed principle. This frontier later came to be known as the MacMahon Line, for Sir Henry MacMahon, Secretary to the Government of India in the Foreign Department, acting as the British Plenipotentiary, had signed it on behalf of His Majesty's Government. As stated above, the Convention was initialed by the plenipotentiaries representing the three governments, but the Chinese refused to proceed to full signature and his government refused to ratify the convention. Britain and Tibet, while signing and ratifying the document, therefore, made a declaration to the effect that "so long as the Government of China withholds signature of the aforesaid Convention she will be debarred from the enjoyment of all privileges accruing therefrom."[11] It may be noted here that some time after the conference China notified Great Britain that except as regards the boundary between Outer and Inner Tibet she agreed to the convention in all respects.[12]

In the following years Sino-Tibetan relations continued more or less on these nebulous foundations. Outer Tibet or Tibet proper remained at least *de facto* independent. China withheld her recognition of the frontier set-up between Inner and Outer Tibet. There were occasional skirmishes (as in 1917, 1931, and 1932) between the Chinese and Tibetan border troops, but on the whole the Tibetans held their own. From time to time there were attempts at negotiations also, but these led to no tangible results.

Mr. Hugh Richardson, who was head of the British Mission at Lhasa from 1936 to 1940 and again from 1946 to 1947, and of the Indian Mission from 1947 to 1950, and who had thus an invaluable opportunity of studying Sino-Tibetan relations from inside Tibet, says: "When the Manchu dynasty collapsed in 1911, Tibet completely severed that link, and until the Communist invasion of 1950, enjoyed *de facto* independence from Chinese control."[13] British official views had also slowly veered round to the position of regarding Tibet as a virtually independent country, although Britain did not go so far as to accord it open diplomatic recognition. Writing to the Counselor of the American Embassy in London in August, 1942, the head of the Far Eastern Department of the British Foreign Office stated: ". . . . *the Tibetans not only claim to be but actually are an independent people,* and they have in recent years fought successfully to maintain their freedom against Chinese attempts at domination." He referred also to the "distinct racial, political, religious and linguistic characteristics" of the Tibetans.[14]

Again on August 5, 1943, Mr. Anthony Eden (now the Earl of Avon), then Secretary of State for Foreign Affairs in the British Government, in the course of a memorandum written to Dr. T. V. Soong, Chinese Minister for Foreign Affairs, stated:

Since the Chinese Revolution of 1911, when Chinese forces were withdrawn from Tibet, Tibet has enjoyed *de facto* independence. She has ever since regarded herself as completely autonomous and has opposed Chinese attempts to reassert control. . . . [Nevertheless, he added, the British] have always been prepared to recognise Chinese suzerainty over Tibet but only on the understanding that Tibet is regarded as autonomous. Neither the British Government nor the Government of India have any territorial ambitions in Tibet but they are interested in the maintenance of friendly relations with, and the preservation of peaceful conditions in, an area which is conterminous with North-

East frontiers of India. They would welcome any amicable arrangements which the Chinese Government might be disposed to make with Tibet whereby the latter recognised Chinese suzerainty in return for an agreed frontier and an undertaking to recognise Tibetan autonomy. . . .[15]

In sum, Tibet in 1950, when Communist China decided to invade and subjugate her, was a nation enjoying *de facto* independence without full *de jure* recognition by the Powers. It is this want of *de jure* recognition, this technical flaw in the status of Tibet, that Communist China decided to exploit so as to make this country a part of the Chinese *lebensraum*.

chapter 3

COMMUNIST CHINA CONQUERS TIBET

MONTHS BEFORE January 1950, when Chou En-lai declared his government's determination to "liberate" Tibet and "stand guard at the Chinese frontiers," the "People's Army" units were already on the march. Thousands of laborers had been pressed into road construction through the difficult mountains. Bridge steel had steadily been moved in barges up the river from Shanghai. Troops were being trained for fighting at high altitudes. In March Tatsienlu in the buffer area between China and Tibet had been captured and since then border incidents in other areas had been engineered to probe the strength of Tibetan resistance.

The Tibetans were naturally alarmed. For over a thousand years they had sought to live a life of religion, apart from the larger movements of the world, and neglected the art of war. And the alarm was ten times greater now than it ever was in the past, for Mao's China had inherited not only the mantle of the Son of Heaven but also the legacy of Marx and Lenin. Chinese imperialism was bad enough; but Chinese imperialism, reinforced by godless Communism, was, in Tibetan eyes, the very antithesis of the values for which they had stood for centuries. Years before the Tibetans had had a foretaste of Chinese Communism. In 1934 the Communist armies of the "long march," escaping battle with Chiang Kai-shek to reach a haven in the interior of China, had crossed into Tibetan-populated Sikang and other areas to the north of Tibet, looted the monasteries, plundered the countryside, destroyed invaluable manuscripts and works of art, and shot down men, women, and children who offered the slightest resistance.[1] "This is our only foreign debt," Mao had said some years later to Edgar Snow, "and some day we must pay the Mantzu and Tibetans for the provisions we were obliged to take from them."[2] Now that Mao was in power, he prepared to repay this "foreign debt" by robbing Tibet of its independence and destroying its way of life.

As China's military build-up against Tibet proceeded apace, disturbing reports began to appear in the Indian press; and although the government could neither confirm nor repudiate them, there is hardly any doubt that deep concern was felt in knowledgeable quarters in the country. Having achieved her freedom only three years before, India instinctively felt some sympathy for peoples struggling to throw off a foreign yoke or attempting to maintain their freedom against external encroachments. And Tibet was not only India's next-door neighbor but linked with India by close cultural and economic ties forged in bygone ages. It was India's Padmasambhara, Dharmapala and Atisa Dipankara who had given to Tibet the major ingredients of her religious and spiritual life. Tibetan script was India's old Brahmi script of the eighth century borrowed and adapted to Tibetan needs. Through the centuries since Tibet adopted Buddhism, there had been a steady stream of pilgrim traffic between the two countries, religious men moving to and fro across the difficult mountain passes to pay worship to their holy shrines. A sizable amount of trade was also carried on between the two since Tibet was opened up by the British in the first decade of this century. Moreover, the new Indian government had inherited from the British certain rights and privileges in Tibet. Would those rights and privileges remain undisturbed if the Chinese subjugated Tibet again? But surpassing all other considerations was the question of Indian security. Could India remain unconcerned while major operations were being undertaken to alter the power structure along her 2,000-mile Himalayan frontier?

In fact, in the middle of 1950 free India was confronted with a problem very similar to the one with which Lord Curzon believed he was confronted in 1904. Not that all Indians understood the implications of the situation. There was a widespread feeling in the country that the Himalayas constituted an impenetrable frontier, and it did not matter much what happened beyond them. The so-called "progressive intellectuals" in some Indian universities told the students that Tibet had always been a part of China, that China had a legal, and now being Communist, also a moral right to do what she chose with the Tibetans, and that there was no reason why India should feel any concern about developments beyond the Himalayas. The government of India, which knew better, was nevertheless of two minds, torn between loyalty toward a weak and helpless neighbor with which India's fundamental interest was linked and loyalty to the old concept of Sino-Indian friendship and a new one of "resurgent Asia" symbolized by Communist China.[3]

In any case, the government of India seems to have instructed its ambassador, K.M. Panikkar, to get in touch with the Chinese leaders to find out what they intended to do about Tibet. On August 22 Panikkar met Chou En-lai. "I expressed the hopes," he writes, "that they [the Chinese] would follow a policy of peace in regard to Tibet. Chou En-lai replied that while the liberation of Tibet was a 'sacred duty', his Government were anxious to secure their ends by negotiations and not by military action."[4]

Meantime the Dalai Lama's government, which knew how

helpless Tibet was in the face of the mounting threat from
China, had sent a seven-man mission led by Mr. Tsepon
Shakabpa to India with a view to making preliminary contacts
with the representatives of the Peking government. The members of the mission, however, made it known that they considered it preferable to meet the representatives of the Chinese
government in some neutral territory such as Hong Kong
rather than in Tibet or China. In fact, they began to prepare
for flying to Hong Kong; but visas for entering Hong Kong
were refused by the British authorities, primarily on the
ground that negotiations such as those projected by the mission
might accentuate the "delicate situation" in that island. China,
however, agreed that the Tibetan delegation might carry on
preliminary negotiations in New Delhi with General Yuan
Chung-shien, the first Chinese Ambassador accredited to the
Government of India.

Some conversations were accordingly held in New Delhi; but
they ended inconclusively on October 1. A spokesman of the
delegation stated that the Chinese Ambassador had declined
to commit himself on the future of Sino-Tibetan relations. At
this stage the Indian government, anxious for a settlement of
the Tibetan question by peaceful negotiations, strongly advised
the Tibetan mission to proceed without delay to Peking for
direct negotiation with the Chinese authorities. The members
of the mission, who knew well enough what it would be like
once they were in the den of the wolf, agreed to the suggestion
since that was the only alternative left to an actual invasion of
Tibet. They got in touch with Lhasa, obtained fresh instruc-
tions, and were in Calcutta on their way to Peking when
India was startled by the news that the Chinese army had
already launced a full-scale invasion of Tibet.

On October 7, 1950, without warning or ultimatum, forty
thousand troops of the 18th and 62nd Chinese armies had
crossed into Tibet at three points and overwhelmed the Tibetan
border forces. On October 19 they captured the Tibetan for-
tress town of Chamdo three hundred miles east of Lhasa. On

October 22 they were in control of Lho Dzong, where the Salween river cuts across the main track to Lhasa. Having thus done a major part of the military job in less than a fortnight, on October 25 Peking announced: "Units of the Chinese People's Army have been ordered to cross over into Tibet in order to free three million Tibetans from Western Imperialist oppression and to consolidate national defences on China's western borders." Past masters in the arts of duplicity, the Chinese raised the false bogey of "Western imperialist oppression" in order to delude the Indian people and exploit their sentiments against Western colonialism in the execution of their design. In fact, the Western powers were so preoccupied with the Korean crisis that they had hardly any time to think of Tibet at the moment. There were not more than two Europeans in Tibet at the time of the invasion— Reginald Fox and Robert Ford, both radio operators. Ford was later arrested by the Chinese and kept in prison for many years. Moreover, geographically, Tibet is so isolated as to make any foreign intervention impossible without the concurrence of India, and India on account of her policy of non-alignment was understandably not willing to provide facilities of the Indo-Tibetan routes for the transport of any foreign military assistance to Lhasa.

From about the second week of August reports of fighting on the borderlands of Tibet began intermittently to appear in the Indian press. They were all discounted by official circles in New Delhi because they ran counter to the assurances which Peking had given to the government of India, and there was no confirmation of the reports from the Indian Ambassador in China. Even as late as October 12, 1950, when *The Statesman* (Calcutta) published a detailed report from its special correspondent in Darjeeling on the Chinese invasion in Tibet, it was characterized by Indian official circles as a "hotch potch story based probably on caravan stories."

The Indian government was, therefore, stunned with surprised when they heard of the Peking announcement of

October 25. On the following day a note was sent to Peking, expressing "surprise" and "regret" at the invasion of Tibet by the Chinese army, and at the fact that China should have sought a solution of the problem of her relations with Tibet "by force instead of by the slower and enduring method of peaceful approach." The surprise was all the greater, the government of India stated, because "we have been repeatedly assured of a desire by the Chinese Government to settle the Tibetan problem by peaceful means and negotiations."

The reply which Peking gave to this note on October 30 was couched in haughty and insulting language. "Tibet is an integral part of Chinese territory," the Chinese note stated. "The problem of Tibet is entirely the domestic problem of China. The Chinese People's Liberation Army must enter Tibet, liberate the Tibetan people and defend the frontiers of China. This is the resolved policy of the Central People's Government." To this was added a stern warning that in the settlement of the Tibetan question "no foreign interference shall be tolerated" and an intimation that the Indian viewpoint about Tibet was "affected by foreign influences hostile to China."[5]

On October 31 the government of India sent another note to Peking, repudiating its allegation that "the Indian viewpoint was affected by foreign influences hostile to China," and expressing the "earnest hope" that a settlement of the Tibetan problem would still "be effected by peaceful negotiations, *adjusting the legitimate Tibetan claim to autonomy within the framework of Chinese suzerainty.*" Peking was assured that the government of India "have no political or territorial ambitions as to Tibet and do not seek any novel privileged position for themselves or for their nationals in Tibet." But, they added,

certain rights have grown out of usage and agreements which are natural between neighbours with close cultural and commercial relations. These relations have found expression in the presence of an agent of the Government of India in Lhasa and the existence of trade agencies at Gyantse for over forty years. The Government of India are anxious that these establishments, which are to the mutual interest of India and Tibet and do not detract in any way from Chinese suzerainty over Tibet, should continue.

The Chinese reply to this note (dated November 16) reiterated the earlier stand that "the Chinese People's Liberation Army must enter Tibet, liberate the Tibetan people and defend the frontiers of China," rebuked the government of India for having "attempted to influence and obstruct the exercise of its sovereign rights in Tibet by the Chinese Government," but held out some kind of vague hope that the problems relating to "Sino-Indian diplomatic, commercial and cultural relations with respect to Tibet may be solved properly and to our mutual benefit through normal diplomatic channels."[6]

While this exchange of notes was going on between New Delhi and Peking, Tibet, like a drowning man catching at every straw, decided to seek the help of the United Nations in a last-minute effort to save herself. Lhasa requested India to sponsor her case. The government of India, however, informed Tibet that she might make a direct appeal to the United Nations, and that they would support her appeal to the extent of condemning China for using force against her. Accordingly on November 7, 1950, the Tibetan government cabled an appeal direct to the Secretary-General of the United Nations, stating that the problem which had arisen "was not of Tibet's own making but largely the outcome of China's ambition to bring weaker nations on her periphery within her active domination." The appeal affirmed that "racially, culturally and geographically" the Tibetans are "far apart from the Chinese."

As a people devoted to the tenets of Buddhism [the appeal went on] Tibetans had long eschewed the art of warfare, practised peace and tolerance and for the defence of their country, relied on its geographical configuration and on non-involvement in the affairs of other nations. There were times when Tibet sought but seldom received the protection of the Chinese Emperor. The Chinese, however, in their urge for expansion, have wholly misconstrued the significance of the ties of friendship and interdependence that existed between China and Tibet as between neighbours. To them China was suzerain and Tibet a vassal state. It is this which aroused legitimate apprehension in the mind of Tibet regarding the designs of China on her independent status.

China's conduct during the expedition of 1910 completed the rupture between the two countries. In 1911-12 Tibet, under the Thirteenth Dalai Lama, declared her complete independence, even as Nepal simultaneously broke away from allegiance to China. The Chinese Revolution in 1911, which dethroned the last Manchu Emperor, snapped the last of the sentimental and religious bonds between China and Tibet. Tibet thereafter depended entirely on her isolation, her faith in the wisdom of the Lord Buddha, and occasionally on the support of the British in India for her protection.

The appeal finally mentioned the invasion of Tibet by Chinese forces at a time when "negotiations were proceeding," and asserted: "This unwarranted act of aggression has not only disturbed the peace of Tibet, but is in complete disregard of the solemn assurance given by the Chinese to the Government of India."[7]

On November 15 El Salvador filed a request that the Tibetan appeal be put on the agenda of the General Assembly. Unfortunately for Tibet, most of the important member nations of the U.N. were at this moment preoccupied with the Korean crisis. Britain and the United States made it known, however, that they would follow India's lead in dealing with the Tibet question. But India backed out of the understanding she had given to Tibet at the last moment. Alarmed by the prospect of a general war on the Korean issue, she decided not to worsen the international situation by condemning China in the forum of the United Nations. On November 24, when the request of the El Salvador delegation came up for discussion in the General Committee of the United Nations, Britain, obviously in consultation with India, moved for a postponement of the matter. This was strongly supported by the Jam Saheb of Navanagar, representing India. "The Indian Government," he stated, "was certain that the Tibetan question could still be settled by peaceful means, and that *such a settlement could safeguard the autonomy which Tibet had enjoyed for several decades* while maintaining its historical association with China." The members then unanimously voted in favor of adjournment. Ernest Gross of the United States, however, stated that "he had voted for adjournment in view of the fact that the Government of India, whose territory bordered on Tibet and which was therefore an interested party, had told the General Committee that it hoped that the Tibetan question would be peacefully and honourably settled."[8]

The appeal of a weak, friendly country, in the preservation of whose freedom India had a vital interest, was not considered by the United Nations at the intervention of the Indian government. The hope which India held out that "the autonomy which Tibet had enjoyed for several decades" would be safeguarded did not materialize. A peaceful neighbor was, in effect, sacrificed to appease the bully.

During these fateful weeks when notes were being exchanged between India and China and the Tibet appeal was before the United Nations, the People's Government at Peking had been pouring fresh reinforcements of troops into Tibet and occupying Tibetan outposts along the country's northwestern and southeastern frontiers. Confronted with utter annihilation, abandoned by the world, the Dalai Lama's government had now no other recourse left but to come to terms with China. Late in April, 1951, a six-man Tibetan delegation arrived at Peking and on May 23 it signed a 17-clause agreement popularly known as the Sino-Tibetan Agreement of 1951. Under its terms the Tibetans agreed to "unite and drive out imperialist, aggressive forces from Tibet so that the Tibetan people could return to the big family of the Motherland—the People's Republic of China." They also agreed to the establishment of a Military and Administrative Committee and a Military Area Headquarters in Tibet. Peking was to take control of Tibetan external affairs, trade, and communications. The Tibetan army was to be absorbed in the People's Liberation Army. In return, Peking promised not to alter the existing political system in Tibet or change the established status, functions, and powers of the Dalai Lama or effect any change in the religious beliefs, customs, and habits of the Tibetan people or the income of the monasteries.

Tibet thus lost not only her *de facto* independent status, but also the autonomy which she had generally enjoyed under the Manchus. Besides obtaining full control over trade, communications, and external affairs of Tibet, China acquired the right to maintain as large an army as she might desire within Tibetan territories so as to keep the country under virtual military occupation. In fact, what emerged out of the agreement was not the "legitimate Tibetan autonomy within the framework of Chinese suzerainty," as the government of India wanted, but full-fledged Chinese sovereignty over Tibet, with restricted Tibetan rights to autonomy in certain limited spheres.

But the agreement was a *diktat*. As the Dalai Lama stated at Mussoorie on June 20, 1959, it was "thrust upon the people and Government [of Tibet] by threat of arms. It was never accepted by them of their own free will. Consent of the Government was secured under duress and at the point of the bayonet."

My representatives [the Dalai Lama added], were compelled to sign the agreement under the threat of further military operations against Tibet by invading armies of China leading to the utter ravage and ruin of the country. . . . While I and my Government did not voluntarily accept that agreement, we were obliged to acquiesce in it and decided to abide by its terms and conditions in order to save my people and my country from the damages of total destruction.

India looked on while this grim tragedy was enacted at her doorstep. The idealism, strength, and resourcefulness with which Prime Minister Nehru sought to rouse the world conscience in 1949 when the Dutch renewed their aggression in Indonesia were inexplicably absent in his handling of the Tibetan question. Yet the issues involved in both cases were fundamentally the same; two neighoring nations, who had known through bitter experience what foreign domination meant, were in dead earnest to make or keep themselves free. Prime Minister Nehru had deep human sympathy for the Tibetans and, as already stated, was anxious that the problem of Sino-Tibetan relations should be settled through peaceful negotiations and not by force. Speaking to the Indian Parliament on December 6, 1950, he stated that since the People's Government of China had declared its intention to "liberate" Tibet, the Indian Ambassador in Peking was instructed to inform the Chinese about Indian feelings in the matter. "We told them we earnestly hoped that this matter would be settled peacefully by China and Tibet," and that while we did not deny Chinese suzerainty, we were equally "interested in maintaining Tibetan autonomy." "It is not clear to me," he added, "from whom the Chinese were going to liberate Tibet." On the day following, replying to the debate on foreign affairs in the Parliament, he went a step further and said: ". . . it is a right and proper thing to say, and I see no difficulty in saying it to the Chinese Government that whether you have suzerainty over Tibet or sovereignty over Tibet, surely, according to any principles, the principles you proclaim and the principles I proclaim, the last voice in regard to Tibet should be the voice of the people of Tibet".[9] These were noble sentiments, expressed by one of the greatest leaders of the contemporary world. But mere enunciation of principles, without the readiness to see that they were implemented, was of little practical use.

But something more was at stake in the Tibet question than mere principle. The British policy of maintaining Tibet as a buffer in past generations was not in the main a product of either British whim or imperialist plot. With the partition of India on the one hand and the emergence of a powerful, centralized, Communist state in mainland China on the other, the importance of that policy had increased rather than lessened. There is no reason to think that Nehru was completely unaware of the implications of a Chinese-occupied Tibet. Replying to a debate in the Indian parliament in 1959, he stated: "Right from the beginning of 1950, or at any rate from 1951 when the Chinese forces came into Tibet, we have had this problem [of Indian security] before us. . . . Looking through my old papers I am surprised myself to see how we had referred to this contingency nine or ten years ago in our papers." Yet he took few effective steps to forestall the oncoming contingency.

Why he did not do so it is not easy to say. The state papers essential to an understanding of the considerations governing the actions of the various nations during this complex period are still buried in the secret files of governments. The apologists of the government of India's policy (or want of policy) point to the staggering internal problems of the country, the essential need for peace to build up the Indian economy, and the continuing strained relations between India and Pakistan, and contend that in view of these circumstances there was nothing better that India could have done. Few will doubt the validity of these premises; but there may still be room for disagreement on the validity of the conclusion. If India was relatively weak, China had her hands full with the Korean war. If India's relations with Pakistan were far from friendly, there were other nations from whom she could have secured friendly support. In fact, contemporary press reports suggest that both Great Britain and the United States would not have been unwilling to stand by India in case she decided to adopt a stronger policy on the Tibet question.

Some commentators have stressed the difficulties of communication between India and Tibet; but India provides the easiest and most convenient avenue to and from Central Tibet, as the Chinese themselves have found. In 1912 Chinese garrisons in Tibet had to be evacuated through Indian territory because it was much easier to travel to China through India than through the mountainous terrain of Inner Tibet. In 1953 the Chinese army in Tibet and the famishing Tibetan people had to be fed with supplies sent through India. Geographical conditions, therefore, did not make it impossible for India to adopt a more positive policy toward the Tibetan question in 1950.

There were excellent historical reasons to repudiate the Chinese claim that Tibet was an integral part of Chinese territory or that her affairs were exclusively China's concern. Tibet's history since the beginning of this century shows that fundamental matters affecting her were regarded even by China as proper subjects for tripartite consultations between herself, Tibet, and Britain. The Simla conference of 1913-14 provided the most typical example of such tripartite consultations. The convention resulting from the conference, to which India was a party, had guaranteed the territorial integrity of Outer Tibet. Under Article 2 of the convention the government of China engaged not to convert Tibet into a Chinese province; under Article 3 they further engaged not to send troops into Outer Tibet, or to station civil or military officers there, or to establish Chinese colonies in the country. True, the convention was not ratified by China, but as stated before, the only ground mentioned by the Chinese government for their refusal to ratify the convention related to the question of the Sino-Tibetan frontier, not to the other clauses of the treaty. It was possible, therefore, for India to take her stand on the Simla convention and plainly tell China that she could not agree to any alteration of the *status quo* in Tibet by the unilateral action of China. If the position was to be reviewed or revised, it should be done through negotiations between China, Tibet, and India as at the Simla conference. Moreover, in reply to the Chinese note of October 30, 1950, in which Peking stated that in the settlement of the Tibetan question "no foreign interference will be tolerated," she might have told China point-blank that both legally and historically India had a better right to take an interest in Tibet than China had in Korea. And then to convince Peking that she meant business, she might have roused the conscience of the world in favor of Tibet, canvassed the necessary diplomatic and other support, and even gone to the extent of making a show of force.

Whether such a posture of strength would have had any effect on Chinese policy is not certain. But Chinese soldiers were already engaged on the Korean front, and prudence might have dictated a policy of moderation on the south-western frontier. But not only was no such policy attempted; India did not even stick firmly to the line so categorically stated by Mr. Anthony Eden in his memorandum of 1943 to Dr. Soong. It is a pity that Indian recognition of Chinese suzerainty over Tibet was at no time unequivocally stated to be dependent upon Chinese recognition of complete Tibetan autonomy. Not that India felt no concern about it; the Indian notes sent to Peking in the last week of October, 1950, make it abundantly clear that she was anxious about the continuance of Tibetan autonomy. But she never made it a precondition of her recognition of Chinese suzerainty. The conclusion thus seems to be irresistible that India wrote off Tibet from her defense calculations, and decided to lean on Sino-Indian friendship for the security of her northern frontier. Conversely, it may be stated that the Chinese policy of aggression against Tibet was based on the sure knowledge that India would not stand in their way.

Why India decided to keep out of the path of Communist China is, as stated above, not easy to determine. Perhaps her Asianism—Prime Minister Nehru was thinking in terms of a third bloc of Asian powers in 1950—and her obsession with

Western colonialism blurred her vision to an extent which made it impossible for her to see that while Western colonialism was passing through a process of retrocession, a new type of totalitarian imperialism was fast taking shape, threatening the liberties of individuals and of nations, great and small. Led astray by this obsession and swayed by this sentiment, India was perhaps a little too prone to believe in the justice of the Chinese claims and the ultimate righteousnss of Chinese intentions. She gambled away Tibet possibly in the belief that the Chinese were not actuated by any aggressive designs but were only acting to reestablish their "historic" association with Tibet. Perhaps India feared that any posture of strength on her part on the Tibet issue would rouse the wrath of the entire Communist world against her and bring her policy of non-alignment to an untimely end. Possibly also in the fall of 1950 she was more appalled by the spectre of a world war on the Korean issue than by the dangers which might accrue from the Chinese conquest of Tibet. Panikkar's chapter on Korea (in his *In Two Chinas*) leaves no doubt in one's mind that in the crucial months of 1950 he was primarily concerned with the Korean question. The Chinese invasion of Tibet, which occurred on October 7, but of which, in spite of his friendliness with Chinese leaders, he knew nothing until it was broadcast by the Peking radio on October 25, was in his eyes of minor and insignificant importance. In other words, in trying to save the peace of the world, India sacrificed an unarmed neighboring country and along with it her own vital interests.

chapter 4

INDIA FACES CHINA IN TIBET

WHATEVER be the motivation of its policy, in 1950, with Tibet under Chinese Communist occupation, the government of India was inevitably filled with a new sense of concern about its long Himalayan frontier. This frontier had for centuries been "dead" to all intents and purposes, but who could guarantee its continuing "dead" in the years to come? One of the bases of Sino-Indian friendship had been the physical distance between the two countries. Now with the distance annihilated, who could tell what the future held in store?

Superficially viewed, the problem which the government of India confronted in 1950 was in a way similar to the problem faced by the old British Government in India in 1910 when a Chinese army invaded and, for a short time, occupied Tibet. But in reality it was very different in character and significance. In 1910 China was still weak and fragmented. In 1950 it had been transformed into a monolithic totalitarian state with its immense manpower and resources organized, regimented and mobilized in support of the revolutionary goals set by the leaders of the regime. Unaware or half aware of the implications of the situation, the government of India decided to employ the same technique used by the British in 1910: to strengthen the inner line of defense constituted by the Himalayas and the frontier Himalayan states of Bhutan, Sikkim, and Nepal.

From the northeastern tip of Kashmir to Namcha Barwa on the northeastern frontier of Assam, India's northern border with Tibet extends over a distance of more than 2,000 miles. Along the easternmost part of it, on the Indian side of the border, lies the North-East Frontier Agency (usually abbreviated into NEFA). To the west of NEFA are the three hill-states of Bhutan, Sikkim, and Nepal, jointly having a frontier of about 1,000 miles with Tibet. And to the west and northwest of Nepal, bordering on Tibet, lie the four Indian states of Uttar Pradesh, Panjab, Himachal Pradesh, and Kashmir including Ladakh. The government of India now directed its attention to strengthening the defensibility of each of these frontier areas.

The NEFA, which lies along the Indo-Tibetan border in the northeast, is a large submontane region extending in length for about 300 miles and in depth between 70 and 150 miles. The MacMahon Line follows the main Himalayan crest behind the submontane tract. The submontane tract itself is rugged, mountainous terrain, covered with deep forests, inhabited by a number of savage tribes, among whom the Abors and the Mishmis are the most prominent. Following the Chinese invasion of Tibet in 1910, the British had carried out extensive explorations in this little-known region and brought the tribes under a loose but efficient control. Faced now with a similar situation, the Indian government embarked upon a more thoroughgoing policy of extending political and administrative control over the tribes, set apart large sums for the development of the area, building roads and airstrips, schools and hospitals, and established army units at strategic points along the frontier.[1] When in November, 1950, Nehru's attention was drawn to the Chinese maps which showed the whole of the submontane tract and even parts of the Brahmaputra valley of Assam as belonging to China, the Prime Minister unequivocally stated: "The MacMahon Line is our boundary, map or no map. We will not allow anybody to come across that boundary."[2]

Bhutan, sometimes described as the Land of the Thunder Dragon, was and is a more sensitive area than NEFA. It comprises an area of about 18,000 square miles along the southern slopes of the Himalayas and a population of some 700,000, who are of Tibetan stock and look upon Lhasa as their spiritual home and the Dalai Lama as their spiritual head. China has always regarded the Mongolian peoples that border on her own and Tibetan frontiers, the Bhutanese, the Sikkimese, and the Nepalese, are rightfully belonging to her sphere of influence. Bhutan, in particular, was considered as "the gate on the south." Strategically, it commands some of the richest areas of Bengal and Assam, including the tea gardens of the Dooars. All through history, it has provided routes for an easier and quicker communication between India and Central Tibet than those now in general use. Moreover, Bhutan's climate and its comparatively fertile valleys are in many ways ideal for colonization by the Chinese from southern and central China. The British, who knew the implications of Bhutan for the safety of India, had by a treaty in 1910 taken Bhutanese foreign relations under their control in return for an annual subsidy. Lest there be any doubt about the validity of that treaty after India became independent, on August 8, 1949, the government of India entered into a new treaty with Bhutan under the terms of which Bhutan agreed "to be guided by the advice of the Government of India in regard to its external relations" in return for an annual subsidy of 500,000 rupees.

With Sikkim, strategically situated on the main trade route between Tibet and India, the Indian government similarly entered into a fresh treaty on December 5, 1950, under the terms of which India acquired not only full control of Sikkim's external relations, but also the right to take such measures as she considered necessary for the defense of Sikkim or the security of India, whether preparatory or otherwise, including the right to station troops anywhere in Sikkim. India further acquired the exclusive right of "constructing, and regulating the use of railways, aerodromes and landing grounds" and other communication facilities in Sikkim. Shortly after the conclusion of the treaty, an Indian Dewan was appointed in Sikkim and under his guidance extensive administrative, land, and tax reforms were introduced in the state so as to strengthen its internal stability.

With Nepal, the largest and the most important of the three border hillstates lying between India and Tibet, India had to evolve a new policy with great caution and circumspection. Britain had recognized Nepal's status as an independent kingdom in a treaty of 1923 but had continued to maintain a kind of veiled tutelage over the mountain kingdom. Nepal's independence was, however, recognized by the United States in 1947 and by France in 1949. Independent India also recognized Nepal's independence in a treaty concluded in 1950. But the occupation of Tibet by Communist China brought home to the government of India, perhaps more than ever before, the interdependence of Nepal and India in the matter of defense against any aggression from the north. Speaking to the Indian Parliament in December, 1950, Prime Minister Nehru stated:

Our interest in the internal conditions of Nepal has become still more acute and personal, because of the developments across our frontiers, to be frank, especially those in China and Tibet. Besides our sympathetic interest in Nepal, we are also interested in the security of our own country. From time immemorial the Himalayas have provided us with a magnificent frontier. Of course, they are not as impassable as they used to be, but are still effective. The

Himalayas lie mostly on the northern borders of Nepal. We cannot allow that barrier to be penetrated because it is the principal barrier to India. Therefore, much as we appreciate the independence of Nepal, we cannot allow anything to go wrong in Nepal or permit that barrier to be crossed or weakened, because that would be a risk to our own security.

Almost four years later, speaking to a press conference at New Delhi on November 13, 1954, Nehru restated Indian policy toward Nepal in the following words: ". . . so far as Nepal is concerned, it is a well-known fact—and it is contained in our treaties and other engagements with Nepal—that we have a special position in Nepal—not interfering with their independence but not looking with favour on anybody else interfering with their independence either."

There is hardly any doubt that the Chinese occupation of Tibet filled India with a new sense of urgency regarding the internal conditions of Nepal, and impelled her to do all she could to help in promoting peace, stability, and orderly progress in the northern kingdom. At crucial moments in Nepalese affairs Indian advice and intervention were sought and freely given. Extensive financial assistance was also extended for development purposes. In addition to an annual subsidy of $200,000, India extended a loan of $350,000 in 1952, and such financial assistance has continued ever since. Moreover, Indian army engineers were sent to Nepal to help in the construction of motor roads between Katmandu and India, and other Indian experts to train the Nepalese army and civil service and set up schools. In short, it became a primary objective of Indian policy to set up Nepal as a progressive, stable, friendly state so that it might serve as an effective bulwark against infiltration or invasion from the north.

To keep watch along the frontier to the west and northwest of Nepal, particularly along the routes through the Himalayan range, the government of Uttar Pradesh created a special constabulary force with the help of the central government, while the latter placed small army units to guard the border between Ladakh and western Tibet.

All these formed only one side of the new policy toward China since 1950. The other side of the new policy was to befriend China, woo and appease her, so as to induce her to follow a policy of moderation in regard to Tibet and refrain from posing a threat along India's Himalayan frontier. This is one of the reasons, although by no means the only one, why India became one of the foremost spokesmen for the views and rights of Communist China in the world forum. Year after year she took the lead in pressing Peking's claim to China's seat in the United Nations. To placate Communist China she refused to recognize the Nationalist Government in Formosa. Nehru went out of his way to criticize the United States for her non-recognition of Communist China and repeatedly urged the powers to accept "the facts of political life" in East Asia as he understood them.

The role which India played in the Korean war bears the same impress of a desperate anxiety to keep on the right side of China. When the war broke out in June, 1950, India supported the United Nations resolution condemning North Korea as an aggressor and calling for a cease-fire and withdrawal of the northern forces from South Korea. But when Communist China began to show resentment against the steady advance of the United Nations forces, the Indian attitude underwent a marked change. In fact, India almost identified herself with the Chinese view that the crossing of the 38th parallel amounted to a direct threat to the security of China, and if Peking had sent its forces into North Korea, it had done so in sheer self-defense. It is, therefore, no wonder that when in February, 1951, a resolution was moved in the United Nations General Assembly condemning Chinese aggression in Korea, India voted with the Soviet bloc against the resolution. A few months later (May 18) India also refused to participate in the United Nations General Assembly vote which imposed an arms embargo against Communist China and North Korea. One may detect the same anxiety to woo China in the Indian attitude toward the San Francisco conference held in September, 1951, for the signing of the Japanese peace treaty. Among the reasons which India put forward in support of her refusal to participate in the conference, one was that the treaty was being signed without the participation of China, which should take part in any settlement of Far Eastern affairs, and another that there was no provision in the treaty to restore Formosa to China. It seems rather extraordinary that few Indian leaders realized that it was not in India's interest to see a strong China, entrenched along her frontier, become stronger by the incorporation of Formosa and all that it implied. It was natural, however, that Communist China, which characterized the Japanese treaty as a war pact, should make capital out of New Delhi's views.

Another aspect of Indian policy of promoting friendship with China was the institution of "cultural exchanges"—delegations of all kinds, good-will, cultural, student youth, trade-union, and even judicial—going from one country to the other. The delegations from the Indian side were often of a miscellaneous sort. But they generally included a fair proportion of men and women who went on their mission with a zeal and devoutness reminiscent of pilgrims going to holy places. Regarding the leader of one of these delegations, it has been said by a fellow delegate that he was such "a sweet and unsophisticated soul" that he "felt like kneeling down, kissing the Chinese earth and like the giant Antaeus, gaining faith and strength from the common mother."[3]

On their arrival in China, the delegates were ceremoniously received and sumptuously fed. They were taken around the country in conducted tours. But they had few opportunities of meeting or talking to the common man except under official surveillance and through official translators. This did not prevent them from forming their unhesitating conclusions, and on their return home, giving expression to them through the press and on the platform. One delegate described Kuomintang China as "an inferno more horrible and hellish than anything conceived in the nightmares of Dante and Milton", but portrayed New China as a land of superheroes and super-heroines, "steadily and sturdily marching towards a planned goal of scientific perfection." Some spoke of Communist China's unstinted devotion to peace—in spite of Tibet and Korea;[4] others of the wonderful "tolerance" of the new regime —at a time when according to the Chinese Communists themselves millions of non-Communists were being liquidated in China.[5] Some patriotically thought "that China has unquestionably established herself as the leader of Asia and no power on earth will be able to shake her from the position that she undoubtedly deserves".[6] And nearly all sang in praise of the amazing all-round progress that Communist China had made in the short space of two or three years. The general propaganda line of some of these returning pilgrims was: "Chinese achievements are truly amazing. New China's record is unbelievable . . . but mostly so from our own viewpoint and our own miserable national standard of achievement under Congress regime."[7] Interspersed through many of these writings and speeches were disparaging remarks regarding the democratic or the Gandhian technique of solving the nation's problems and an implied preference for the Communist way. "We need the China way of doing things," exclaimed a well-known editor, swept away by the current of pro-China feelings.[8]

Sardar K. M. Panikkar, the well-known diplomat-historian of India, who was Indian Ambassador at Peking at this time, joined his powerful voice to this chorus of praise. In fact, he may be said to have set the tune. "Watching Panikkar," writes Frank Moraes, "I could not help feeling that his sense of history had overwhelmed him. He saw himself projected into the drama of a great revolution, and its excitement had infected him."[9] The infection had indeed gone so far as to transform him, in the opinion of some, into a "Chinese megaphone." He spent long hours in explaining and interpreting New China to the members of these delegations, and no Chinese could have done the job better than he did. Explaining the liquidation of anti-Communists in China, Panikkar said to Moraes: "When after the blow-up in Korea, the American Seventh Fleet was interposed between Formosa and the Chinese mainland and there was talk of an invasion of China, Mao struck." "Did the number of those executed run over two million?" "Possibly, though I think the actual figure was less."[10]

To Sunderlal, who had imbibed something of the Gandhian abhorrence of violence, the Ambassador's interpretation was different. "None of these was shot," he said. "They were disarmed and given two to three years time to improve themselves and become good citizens of the New People's Republic, whereafter their arms could also be restored to them. . . . When it is said that several million soldiers of Chiang Kai-shek were 'liquidated,' the meaning is that they were disarmed and put out of action."[11]

On the conquest of Tibet by China, the versatile Ambassador came forward with a version which is almost Goebbelian in its distortion of historical facts. Tibet, he said, had become a part of China "as early as the eighth century." "The present Dalai Lama was actually appointed by the Chinese Government. . . . When the People's Republic of China was established in 1949, representatives of Tibet were present at all functions in Peking and took part in drawing up New China's 'Common Programme.' "[12] Prime Minister Nehru, as already mentioned, had stated in the Indian Parliament that he did not know "from whom the Chinese were going to liberate Tibet." His Ambassador at Peking professed that he knew. The "British and American intrigues in Tibet against the interests of both Tibet and China were ripening and preparations were afoot to make Tibet a base against China and the

Soviet Union. . . . It was high time for China, in the interest of Tibet as well as her own safety, to take steps for the liberation of Tibet as it had done for the rest of the Chinese territory."[13] This is what the *New China News Agency* had stated some months earlier (September, 1949). But the Agency had included Nehru also in the plot. In fact, he was described as the "running dog" who had joined the "Anglo-American imperialists" in "plotting a *coup* in Lhasa for the annexation of Tibet."[14] One wonders whether the Indian Ambassador believed in this part of the story also.

The nimble-minded Ambassador was ready with an answer for everything—even for the lack of numerical or statistical data which some members of the Indian delegations sought but did not get. K. T. Shah, for instance, complained that "whether it was a question of average holdings, yields per acre, university curricula, student activities or the most elementary banking business," he found himself frustrated by absence of answers, inconsistent answers, or referral to higher authority in Peking. The Indian Ambassador replied that since foreign capitalists had been excluded altogether, the Chinese had only to "inform, instruct and educate their own people," who, "seeing the magnitude and complexity of the tasks being tackled and accomplished, could easily dispense with the aid of statistics, in preference to the evidence of their own eyes!"[15] Returning to India late in 1951 in the company of a Chinese cultural delegation, Panikkar carried on this campaign of glamorizing Communist China in the press and on platform. Communist revolution in China, he said, "was a part of the great Asian resurgence," and Communist China "was not really communist." When his attention was drawn to the large influx of Chinese troops in Tibet, he saw no reason why India should worry about it. "I do not think," he said, "there is anything wrong in the troops of Red China moving about in their own territory."[16]

Not that all Indian visitors to China joined this paean of

praise. Some felt deeply disturbed by what they saw, and struck discordant notes.[17] By and large, the Indian nationalist press also refused to swallow these sentimental and misleading reports. But the general atmosphere created in the country, particularly among the young intelligentsia, was one of admiration, if not adoration, of Communist China. India-China Friendship Associations grew like mushrooms all over the country, and Communists and fellow travelers found a congenial soil to carry on their proselytizing work among the youth of India.

Peking played its cards with dexterous skill. It seemed wise from the Chinese Communists' point of view to secure Indian cooperation in as many international problems as possible through the manipulation of Indian belief in "Sino-Indian friendship" and "Asian solidarity." Indian gestures also opened up new prospects of conversion or subversion; why not take advantage of them? In response to Indian invitations Chinese good-will and cultural missions were sent to India. Exhibitions of Chinese art were held in some big Indian cities. In one of these exhibitions, held at Bombay, a message from Mao Tse-tung was prominently displayed in the exhibition hall. It read: ". . . The Indian people are an excellent people. . . . India, China and the Soviet Union must unite with other peace-loving countries to strive for peace in the Far East and the whole world." China's obvious game was to drive a wedge between India and the West and draw the former into the Communist camp. To promote this objective, she began to distribute in collaboration with the Indian Communists a vast amount of pro-Chinese literature —books, journals, pamphlets, and in particular, Mao Tse-tung's writings in English and Indian translations—at fantastically low prices.

To make a deeper impression on the Indian mind, in 1951 when India was suffering from acute food shortage, Peking dramatically offered to send one million tons of grain. This was advertised by Indian Communist agencies and in the pro-Communist press as a free gift made by the Chinese as a token of "unselfish and sincere friendship for the Indian people" and as a proof that the Communists had already solved the food problem of China. In fact, only 507,702 tons of grain reached India from China during the whole of 1951 and the first four months of 1952, after hard bargaining had resulted in the conclusion of intergovernmental sales agreements. In the same period the United States shipped 3,800,000 tons of grain to India at prices appreciably below those of China. But whereas the United States considerably marred the effect of this help by initial diplomatic bungling, Communist propaganda scored a great triumph by holding up China as a friend in need.

Chinese gestures of good will were, however, interspersed with reservations. A Chinese cultural mission to India in 1951 canceled its proposed visit to Kashmir because of the asylum given by Kashmir government to Kazakh refugees from Tibet. When in December, 1952, India attempted to bring about a Korean truce, Peking poured unmitigated scorn upon Indian proposals and accused India of allying herself with "the Anglo-American camp." The Peking radio commented: "The Indian delegate stated without one reason that he spoke as a representative of the people of Asia. However, no one except the U.S.-dominated bloc has given the Indian delegate such authority."[18]

Nor did China hesitate to squeeze India slowly out of some of her traditional positions in Central Asia and Tibet. Before the Communist victory in China, India used to maintain a consulate general in Kashgar in Sinkiang. The Communists now declared Sinkiang as a "closed area," refused India permission to maintain the consulate in Kashgar, and thus practically stopped all Indian trade with Central Asia. In Tibet the Chinese troops steadily increased in numbers, and by the end of 1951 a virtual military control of the country was estab-

lished. They established a military and administrative headquarters in Lhasa, and undertook the construction of a series
of roads and airstrips and a radio network linking all important towns and districts with the capital. At the same time a
kind of steady pressure was exerted to eliminate, step by step,
all Indian influence in Tibet. Indian visitors and traders in
Tibet were subjected to progressively increasing scrutiny and
hardship. The government of India was pressed to withdraw
its Political Agent from Lhasa, and in September, 1952, the
Political Agency was actually transformed into a consulate
general at Chinese bidding. In fact, it came to be increasingly
realized by India that under the new set-up in Tibet, there
was hardly any alternative but to agree to a revision and re-
definition of her treaty rights in that country.

Negotiations for that purpose were begun at the end of
1953, and it was estimated that six weeks would be enough to
complete them. But they went on for four months. Anxious
inquiries were made in the Parliament; and although the
government vouchsafed no specific information, it soon tran-
spired that the main obstacle in the way of the agreement was
the Chinese insistence "on matching trade agency for trade
agency. India had three trade agencies in Tibet: China now
wanted three trade agencies in India in addition to her embassy in New Delhi and consulates in Calcutta and Bombay.
Suggested new locales for Chinese offices were Almora and
Simla."[19] Both these two places were in the heart of the border
hills adjoining Tibet, and the news was received with great
misgivings in Indian political circles. In the end, an additional
trade agency had to be conceded to the Chinese, not in
Almora or Simla, but at New Delhi, and on April 29, 1954,
representatives of the two governments signed an Agreement
on Trade and Intercourse between the Tibet region of China
and India.

The preamble to the agreement stated that it was based on
the principles of "mutual respect for each other's territorial

integrity and sovereignty, mutual non-aggression, mutual non-interference in each other's internal affairs, equality and mutual benefit, and peaceful co-existence"—principles which were soon christened as the famous *Panch Shila* of Indian foreign policy—and that it was intended to promote trade and cultural intercourse between the "Tibet region of China" and India and to facilitate pilgrimage and travel by the peoples of China and India. The agreement provided for the establishment by China of trade agencies in New Delhi, Calcutta, and Kalimpong, while India was permitted to retain or restore its trade agencies in the Tibetan towns of Yatung, Gyangtse, and Gartok. Markets for trade between the two countries and the six routes which might be followed by pilgrims and traders were specified. Travel regulations were laid down.

Moreover, the notes exchanged between the two governments, which were published with the agreement, provided for the lapsing of those rights and privileges which were exercised by the government of India in Tibet as a result of custom or agreements with the government of Tibet. Thus the government of India agreed (1) to withdraw within six months the military escorts of about 200 men hitherto stationed at Yatung and Gyangtse for the protection of traders and pilgrims, (2) to hand over to the Chinese government at a reasonable price the postal, telegraph, and telephone installations which it operated in Tibet as well as the twelve rest houses which it owned there, and (3) to return to the Chinese government all land and buildings which it used or occupied in Tibet and lease from the Chinese government all land and buildings which it required. The government of India subsequently (April 30, 1954) announced that it had decided that "postal, telegraph and telephone installations together with equipment operated by India in Tibet" were to be transferred "free of cost and without compensation" to the People's Republic of China "as a gesture of goodwill."[20]

Strangely enough, the agreement was greeted with jubilation by most Indian political commentators as a triumph of Indian diplomacy. Chinese acceptance of "mutual respect for each other's territorial integrity" was construed as acceptance, without question, by Peking of the existing frontiers between India and Tibet. The *Panch Shila* was acclaimed as a magic formula which would go a long way toward resolving international difficulties and establishing a "climate of peace" in the world. And since Communist China had sworn by it, it was taken for granted that she could have no evil designs against India. In fact, *Panch Shila* was of no more significance in *realpolitik* than the Kellogg-Briand Pact of the inter-war period—an expression of pious wishes without any sanction behind them.[21] This has been more than proved by the later conduct of China.

In reality, the agreement of 1954 marks an important step in India's withdrawal from Tibet under actual or threatened Chinese pressure. What is extraordinary is that it was now paraded as an act of virtue and international propriety. It will be remembered that in the Indian note that was sent to Peking on October 30, 1950, it was stated that the "rights" which India exercised in Tibet "have grown out of usage and agreements which are natural among neighbours with close cultural and commercial relations" and that the government of India were anxious that those rights, which "do not detract in any way from Chinese suzerainty over Tibet," should continue. But what was considered "natural" in 1950 was condemned in 1954 as "relics of British imperialism." "The British Empire," it was now argued, "in the days of Lord Curzon, about fifty years ago, had expanded into and made several types of arrangements in Tibet. Now it is impossible and *improper* for us to continue any such arrangements as the British Empire had established." But that the Prime Minister was making a virtue of necessity under pressure became evident when he stated: "We must give up these [facilities such as telegraph lines]; if we do not give them up voluntarily, then we *shall be forced* to give them up. . . . The fact is that if we did not like to give up those things, we would have been forced to give them up. We must accept this fact."[22]

But the agreement marked a surrender in other respects also. Under Chinese pressure, India finally abandoned her consulate at Kashgar, thus depriving herself of the advantage of a watch-post in Central Asia. It was this absence of a watch-post that enabled China to construct the Sinkiang-Tibet highway through the Aksai Chin region of Ladakh in 1956-57 without the knowledge of the Indian government.[23] Moreover, again under Chinese pressure, India became a party to the denial to Tibet of its historical and political identity as a nation. For the first time in any diplomatic document Tibet was described in the Sino-Indian agreement of 1954 as the "Tibet region of China." In effect, it amounted to a recognition of Chinese *sovereignty* (instead of suzerainty) over Tibet and of the Chinese right to make it a part of their monolithic state. In return for all these concessions and gestures of good will, India might have at least demanded from China an unequivocal recognition of Indo-Tibetan borders bequeathed to the present by the former government of India. Instead of insisting on any such recognition in terms of the agreement, she preferred to delude herself into thinking that acceptance of the agreement by China meant her acceptance of the frontiers.

The only tangible benefit that India derived from the agreement was the right of continuing her trade with Tibet. But Indo-Tibetan trade was no less important for China than it was for India. From the very outset, however, it was clear that the volume and character of this trade might not remain the same as before. In Communist countries foreign trade is always a state monopoly, and as Khrushchev said some time ago, they "value trade least for economic reasons and most for political purposes." It could thus be foreseen that as soon as China had built her essential communications with Tibet, she might divert Tibetan trade from its traditional southward course. This is what Peking has subsequently done, so that in recent years Indo-Tibetan trade has been reduced to a mere trickle.

"Panch Shila," declared Acharya J. B. Kripalani in the course of a debate in the Lok Sabha four years later, "was born in sin."

"Sind or sin?" inquired Prime Minister Nehru.

"Sin," retorted Kripalani, "because it was enunciated to put the seal of our approval upon the destruction of an ancient nation which was associated with us spiritually and culturally."

Whether born in vice or virtue, it would appear that the Sino-Indian agreement of 1954 (which included the doctrine of *Panch Shila*) was but a logical sequence of the Chinese occupation of Tibet in 1950. Prime Minister Nehru was right when he stated that in the changed context it was no longer possible for India to maintain her old position in Tibet. Certain consequences were bound to follow from the altered power structure across the Himalayas. Elimination of Indian rights was the first of these consequences. Other and more far-reaching consequences were still concealed in the future.

We must not, however, omit to mention one important fact. India was possibly hustled, in some measure, into this agreement by her growing rift with Pakistan and the United States. In August, 1953, when a political conference on Korea was proposed, Pakistan voted in the United Nations in favor of the United States resolution to exclude India from the membership of the conference. In November, 1953, rumors began to be heard that the United States was considering a request from Pakistan for military aid. On November 15, 1953, Prime Minister Nehru expressed intense concern about the reported talks and said that the proposed pact would have far-reaching consequences on the whole structure of things in Asia. On February 24, 1954, in spite of India's known opposition, President Eisenhower announced the decision of the United

States to comply with the request of Pakistan for military aid. This step very decisively affected the Indian attitude toward both Pakistan and the United States. True, in a personal letter, President Eisenhower assured Prime Minister Nehru that the action "is not directed in any way against India." But Indian public opinion was not reconciled. Prime Minister Nehru charged that Pakistan was encircling India by her political and military arrangements; and the press magnified the imminent danger with which India was faced. Viewed in this context, it becomes easy to understand why India was in such a hurry to come to an agreement with China even at the cost of vital interests.

chapter 5

HINDI CHINI BHAI BHAI

THE THREE years following the agreement of April
29, 1954, were years of Sino-Indian honeymoon. Having secured the voluntary elimination of Indian influence from
Tibet as well as Indian support to Chinese aims in the wider
field of international relations, Peking no longer felt any
hesitation in enhancing the tempo of friendship with India.
In fact, friendship with India formed part of a new strategy
which Peking had been steadily evolving since the termination
of the Korean war. Prior to that event, the Chinese Communists, intoxicated by their triumph on the Chinese mainland
and fired by revolutionary zeal, had sought to promote armed
revolts in some of the areas of Southeast Asia. The results
which they produced, however, fell far short of expectation.
The net gain made was the consolidation of Communist rule
in the northern half of Indochina and the integration of North
Vietnam into the Communist bloc. But this had been more
than counterbalanced by the alarm created in the minds of
the governments and peoples of non-Communist Asian countries. It was apprehended in the Communist high command
that unless the tactics were changed, Southeast Asian countries

might be driven by sheer desperation into the arms of the Western bloc. The menaces of Peking toward Thailand in February, 1950, had the effect of inducing that country to abandon her traditional neutral role and align herself firmly with the West.[1]

Peking, therefore, slowly changed its old tactics and evolved a new strategy for dealing with South and Southeast Asian countries. It played down its revolutionary aims, adopted a non-militant, conciliatory posture, and posed as a votary of Asian peace and progress. It proclaimed its faith in "peaceful coexistence," carried on a continuous tirade against Western colonialism and racialism, and bent its efforts to the elimination or at least reduction of Western influence and the corresponding enhancement of Peking's political prestige and economic influence. It promoted exchange of delegations of all kinds—political, labor, commercial, cultural, and good-will —with South and Southeast Asian countries, and sought in various ways to penetrate the region through seemingly innocent activities. In Peking's eyes India was the key to Southern Asia. If the new strategy was to be a success, India's cooperation was essential.

India's attitude toward China was determined, in large measure, by her unrealistic assessment of Chinese leadership. In Nehru's eyes, the supreme need of the moment was peace, particularly in Asia. The only power that might disturb Asian peace was China with her irredentist ambitions. Once those ambitions were satisfied, China, it was believed, would settle down to peaceful internal development. Unfriendly policies would merely antagonize the Chinese Communists and make them belligerent. Friendly policies, on the other hand, would win them over to the cause of peace, stability, and progress and might even make them give up their dependence on the Soviet Union. "A China befriended by India would be a China more amenable to reason"—this appears to have been the assumption on which Indian policy toward China was based through a large part of the decade.

Concern was indeed felt in some political and intellectual circles in the country at the growing hardening of the Chinese attitude in world affairs since 1956. Men of discrimination noted with anxiety how Peking gave all-out support to Soviet military repression in Hungary in 1956, how it repressed and suppressed Chinese intellectuals after the brief "hundred flowers" episode in 1957, the manner in which it began its campaign of vituperation against Tito, with its emphasis on bloc unity and insistence on the adoption of a harsh, rigid line against "disrupting influences" and "revisionist deviations" (1957-58). It is curious that while to non-Communist Asia, Chou En-lai professed his complete faith in peaceful coexistence, within the Communist world Mao insisted that all communities, parties, and nations must march in goose-step along the orthodox way, and there could be no softness, no tolerance for the deviationists. That there was an obvious contradiction between this rigidity and intolerance within the bloc and professions of tolerance outside was clear to many thinkers in and outside India. But Indian policy-makers did not allow themselves to be ruffled either by these subtle contradictions or by the increasing symptoms of Chinese militancy in world affairs. They continued to believe in Panikkar's thesis that Communist China was primarily Chinese and only remotely Communist, and that if shown consideration and friendship, she would turn out to be a bulwark of peace in Asia. It is no wonder, therefore, that there was enthusiastic cooperation between India and China in the years following the conclusion of the Sino-Indian agreement.

Between June, 1954, and January, 1957, Chou En-lai paid four visits to India. On each occasion he was given a warm welcome wherever he went. He held prolonged discussions with Nehru on international problems, reaffirmed his faith in the *Panch Shila* or the five principles of peaceful coexistence, and paid tributes to India for the "consistent and firm support which the Indian Government and people have been giving them [the Chinese] in their struggle for the complete unification of the Fatherland, and in their struggle for the restoration of China's legal rights in the UN."[2] Nehru paid one visit to China from October 18 to 28, 1954. He too was received with enthusiastic acclamation by the Chinese government and people. As usual Chou En-lai waxed eloquent on the *Panch Shila* or five principles of coexistence. "We believe," he said, "that peaceful co-existence and friendly cooperation between China and India will facilitate the gradual realisation of peaceful co-existence among other Asian countries and the countries of the whole world." He praised Nehru's policy of establishing and extending an "area of peace" in Asia, which he contrasted with that of the "SEATO bloc," and promised China's cooperation in that task. "The friendly cooperation of the 960,000,000 people of India and China," he concluded, "constitutes an important factor in safeguarding peace in Asia and the world."

Nehru in his reply emphasized the past friendship between India and China. "The greatest need of the world today," he said, "is peace, and I am convinced that the people of China, like the people of India, are devoted to the cause of peace. The joint statement issued by Mr. Chou En-lai and myself embodies the five principles which should govern the relationship between countries. These principles lay down the sovereign rule that each country should have freedom and independence and should live its own life in friendship with others, but without any interference from outside."[3]

At the end of 1956, when Chou En-lai again came to India, he referred to the valuable contributions made by India "to bring about peaceful solutions to the wars in Korea and Indo-China," as also to the ceaseless interest she has been taking "on the question of banning Atomic, Hydrogen and other weapons of mass destruction." "The Chinese people", he said, "deem it an honour to have such a great neighbour as India".[4] He was, of course, eloquent in his praise of the *Panch Shila,* and declared that he looked forward to the day "when *Panch Shila* would shine over the entire universe like the sun."

Nehru stressed the international importance of friendship and cooperation between India and China, which between them contained almost half the world's population. "India and China," he added, "had met in South-East Asia 1500 years ago and the whole region was strewn with evidence of the cultural impact of these two countries. They were meeting one another in South-East Asia once again and, as in the past, there was no hostility between them."[5]

Reporting on one of his visits to India to the National Committee of the People's Political Consultative Conference on March 5, 1957, Chou En-lai stated:

There is much we Chinese people can learn from our Indian friends. . . . The enthusiastic welcome given us by the Indian people defies description. . . . Wherever we went we heard the hearty cheer: "Hindi Chini Bhai Bhai" [Indians and Chinese are brothers]. . . . Naturally China and India do not hold, nor can they hold identical views on all questions. . . . But, just as Prime Minister Nehru said during our visit to India, "When we disagree in some matters, it is friendly disagreement, and it does not affect our friendship and cooperation". . . . These talks will further help our two countries . . . to play their roles in the common cause of safeguarding world peace and promoting international cooperation.[6]

Supplementing these intergovernmental contacts, contacts and exchanges of other kinds were actively promoted. A thirty-two-member Indian worker's delegation went to China in May, 1955. Nine of them, however, returned home in a few days, cutting short their tour in protest against attempts at "indoctrination" and the Chinese move to form a Communist-inspired Asian Confederation of Labor. This was followed in June, 1955, by a more pompous cultural delegation comprising about 50 artists representing various schools of dancing and music in India. The delegation was led by Mr. A. K. Chanda, then Deputy Minister for External Affairs. In September a delegation of professors and students from Indian universities went on a visit to Peking and other Chinese cities. In July-September, 1956, another Indian delegation visited China to study Chinese agrarian cooperatives. The delegation expressed the view that cooperative farming was necessary in India from economic as well as social considerations. In the following months and years, delegations of one kind or another continued to proceed to China with almost monotonous regularity, some to study Chinese water conservancy and irrigation work, some to study Chinese steel production in backyard furnaces, and others for sundry similar purposes.

Not only did Peking encourage the visits of these delegations from India and other South-Asian countries, it sent out its own delegations to most of them. Early in 1955 it sent a whole round of cultural exhibitions to India, Pakistan, Burma, and Indonesia. In December of the same year, Madame Soong Ching-ling, Vice-Chairman of the Standing Committee of the National People's Congress of China and wife of the late Dr. Sun Yat-sen, paid an august visit to India and was received with great cordiality and ceremony. In early January, 1956, a Chinese Communist student delegation, headed by the Secretary-General of the All-China Students' Federation, arrived in India to attend the International Geography Seminar at Aligarh Muslim University. In 1955 and 1956 Chinese scientific delegations came to India to attend the meetings of the Indian Science Congress.

More important than these were the diplomatic and quasi-diplomatic gatherings in which India and China joined hands in full partnership. Between April 6 and 10, 1955, an eleven-nation non-official conference was held at New Delhi, in which China participated. The conference adopted a number of resolutions demanding *inter alia* the immediate lifting of the embargo on trade with China, seating Red China on the Security Council, and its recognition by all countries. This was soon (April 18-24) followed by the twenty-nine-nation Asian-African Conference at Bandung, which Nehru and Chou En-lai both attended along with the premiers and foreign ministers of other participating governments. Here Chou played his cards with superb skill, declared that he had come "to seek unity, not to quarrel," that China, although a Communist country, had no desire to spread its ideology and that all that it sought for was normal relations with all Asian and African countries, "particularly her own neighbours on a strict adherence to the principles of co-existence agreed upon between India and China."

Here Communist China's irredentist claims were discussed among top participants and in a few days Mr. V. K. Krishna Menon of India proceeded to Peking to discuss ways and means of solving the Formosa problem. Formosa, Mr. Menon said, was "not just an island, but a symbol of many things, good and bad. Unless they get rid of the problem, they may destroy each other." At Peking (May 12 to 21) he discussed the whole question threadbare with Chou En-lai and other members of the Chinese government, formulated certain proposals, and then went hurrying to Washington to discuss them with President Eisenhower and Secretary of State John Foster Dulles. On his way to Washington Mr. Menon discussed his proposals with Sir Anthony Eden, Mr. Harold Macmillan, and other British cabinet ministers in London and with Mr. Louis St. Laurent and Mr. Lester Pearson in Ottawa.

Indeed, from this time India lent all her moral and diplomatic weight in support of Communist China's claims to Formosa and the offshore islands of Quemoy and Matsu. On February 21, 1955, President Dr. Rajendra Prasad, addressing the budget session of the Parliament, referred to the tension in the Far East, and said: "My Government recognises only one Government of China, that is, the People's Republic, and considers that the claims of the Republic are justified." On March 31, speaking in the debate on the budget demand for grants for the Ministry of External Affairs, Nehru said:

So far as we are concerned, obviously we can have only one broad approach to this problem which flows from the recognition of the People's Government of China. There is nobody who says Formosa is a separate state. Formosa claims to be China, and China claims Formosa to be part of it. But there has been general agreement, very wide agreement on one obvious fact—that the islands of Matsu and Quemoy, off the mainland, are definitely part of the mainland. Any enemy force there is a constant irritation and constant danger. . . . Yet the occupation of Quemoy and Matsu by other forces continues.[7]

Nehru's stand on the question of the offshore islands and Formosa was clear and unequivocal and he went on reiterating this stand time after time in the following months and years. Even after Communist China had violated Indian territorial integrity by constructing the Sinkiang-Gartok road through Ladakh, Nehru's sympathies for Peking on the question of Formosa and the offshore islands remained unshaken. Speaking at his monthly press conference on September 7, 1958, he said: "No country could tolerate an island 12 miles from its shores being used as a base for attack on it. India, therefore, felt that the offshore islands immediately, and later Formosa too, should belong to the People's Republic of China." "But this," he added, "must happen peacefully."[8]

Alongside this support to the irredentist claims of Communist China, India continued with her efforts to seat Peking in the Security Council. "I do not think," Nehru said to the Lok Sabha on March 20, 1956, "that so long as the Chinese People's Republic is not admitted to the United Nations, the situation in East Asia will return to normal." When a proposal was mooted that the China seat in the Security Council be given to India, Nehru turned it down on the ground that it would heighten and not lessen tension. In fact, it looked as though the seating of Communist China in the Security Council had become one of the major objectives of Indian foreign policy; and Indian leaders missed no opportunity to press it whenever

an occasion arose, whether in the forum of the United Nations
or in behind-the-scenes diplomatic negotiations or in public
statements.[9]

All this political and cultural collaboration was further supplemented by bilateral trade agreements. During Nehru's visit
to Peking an agreement was concluded with Peking under
which China would operate an air service to India, while the
Air India International Service then terminating at Hong Kong
would extend to Canton. A few days earlier (October 14, 1954)
a trade agreement between India and China was signed at New
Delhi, valid for an initial period of two years but renewed in
1956 and again in 1958. The agreement led to a steep rise in
trade between the two countries. On January 17, 1956, the
New China News Agency reported that trade between India
and China had increased steadily in the past fifteen months.
India's exports to China had increased ninefold, while imports
from China had increased three and a half times over the pre-
Agreement period. On the other hand, the results of the Sino-
Indian agreement on trade and intercourse with the "Tibet
region of China" proved to be far from satisfactory. In consequence of the various controls and restrictive measures adopted
by China, some of the channels of this old traditional trade with
Tibet began to dry up, and large numbers of Bhotiya in Uttar
Pradesh, who lived on this trade, found their means of livelihood suddenly cut off.

But this was not the only strain disturbing the honeymoon.
Year after year Peking went on publishing maps of China which
showed large chunks of Indian territory along the Himalayan
frontier as falling within the territorial limits of the Chinese
state. The Indian territories thus shown within China included
(1) four of the five divisions of NEFA, (2) some areas in the
north of the state of Uttar Pradesh, and (3) large areas in
eastern Ladakh, which forms part of the state of Jammu and
Kashmir. Besides these, the entire Tashi-gang area of eastern
Bhutan and a considerable slice of territory in northwest
Bhutan were also depicted as Chinese territory. The year-to-

year publication of these maps naturally gave rise to some concern in Indian political circles. When Nehru went to China in October, 1954, he raised the question of these maps with Chou En-lai. Chou replied that "these were really reproductions of old pre-liberation maps," and the People's Government "had had no time to revise them."[10] "The Government of India recognised the force of this argument" and did not pursue the matter further.[11]

In July, 1958, these inflated maps of China were published in the *China Pictorial* and also in the Soviet weekly, *The New Times,* both having world-wide circulation. On August 21, 1958, the government of India addressed a note to the Counsellor of China in India, "drawing the attention of the Government of the People's Republic of China again to this matter."[12] Peking now replied that these maps were doubtless reproductions of old maps, but it had "not yet undertaken a survey of China's boundary, nor consulted with the countries concerned," and pending such survey and consultation, it would "not make changes in the boundary on its own."[13] In other words, Peking reserved to itself the right to declare at any time of its own choosing that the chunks of Indian territory shown in Chinese maps as belonging to China were disputed territories.[14]

What was even more disquieting was the physical intrusion by the Chinese into territories which India had traditionally regarded as her own. Not even three months had passed since the signing of the Sino-Indian agreement on Tibet when China laid claim to a two-square-mile area in the Garhwal district of Uttar Pradesh along the Indo-Tibetan border called Bara Hoti by the Indians and Wu-Je by the Chinese. In the summer of 1955 a party of Chinese actually encamped in the area, which thus became a matter of dispute between the two governments. With a view to allaying public suspicion in India, the government of India issued a press note on November 11, 1955, stating that Bara Hoti was of no strategic or other importance, that it lay at an altitude of over 16,000 feet, and that it was mostly uninhabitable. The press note added: "The Indo-

Western sector of the India-China frontier.

Tibetan border is well defined. The question is merely one of fact, namely whether this small area of Bara Hoti lies north or south of the border pass. It is admitted by both sides that if the area is north of the border pass, it would be in Tibet; and if it is south, it would be in India." The Chinese, however, later on went back on this understanding, and claimed Bara Hoti (Wu-Je) as their own, no matter whether it was north or south of the border pass.

Reports of violation of Indian territorial integrity in other

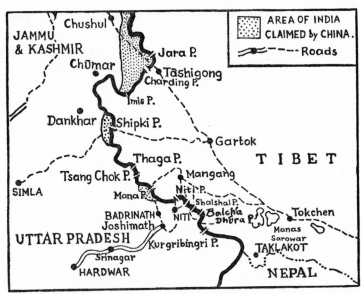

Central sector of the India-China frontier.

border areas also soon began to reach New Delhi. On November 5, 1955, the government of India complained to the Chinese Counsellor in India that a party of twenty Chinese soldiers had trespassed into a place called Damzan, which "is ten miles south of the Niti Pass which has been recognised by the Sino-Indian Agreement of 29th April, 1954, as the border pass between the two countries in this region."[15] On May 2, 1956 another complaint was lodged that twelve Chinese soldiers "including one officer equipped with tommy and sten guns were seen half a mile east of Nilang . . . on 29th April." "Nilang and the area right up to Tsang Chokla pass," the Indian note added, "is clearly within Indian territory and has always been in our possession."[16] A third complaint was lodged on September 8 and repeated September 24, 1956, that a party of about ten Chinese army personnel "entered and took up positions about 2 furlongs from Hupsong Khad on the Indian side of Shipki La Pass," threw stones and threatened to use their grenades against the Indian patrol guarding the border.[17] These complaints went on multiplying as time passed. In October, 1958, the government of India received information that Chinese military personnel had "established outposts" at two other places along the Indo-Tibetan border called Lapthal and Sangcha Malla, "which are both on the Indian side of the Balcha Dhura Pass, which is considered as traditional boundary between India and China." In a note handed to the Chinese Counsellor in India on December 10, 1958, the government of India stated:

These places have never before been claimed either by the Government of China or by the local authorities in the Tibet region of China. The Government of India have been maintaining Indian check-posts at these two places for several years. Due to climatic conditions these check-posts retire further south at the end of the summer months. The Government of India have been informed that when the check-posts retired as usual in October this year, the Chinese personnel entered into Indian territory and established outposts at both the places.[18]

Intrusions of this nature occurred also in other sectors along the frontier. In July, 1958, the Indian government received information that the Chinese troops had intruded into the Ladakh region of Kashmir and occupied India's Khurnak Fort.[19] Information was also received that on September 27-28 another detachment of Chinese troops, approximately fifty strong, had "crossed into the Lohit Frontier Division of the North-East-Frontier Agency of India."[20] But earlier than either of these, and certainly more serious than both, was the violation of Indian territorial integrity involved in the construction of a great Chinese highway through northeastern Ladakh. Taking advantage of the high altitude of Aksai Chin[21] (that was the traditional name of this part of Ladakh), its remote and utterly desolate character, and of the absence of any Indian consulate at Kashgar, the Chinese carried through the construction of this motor road called the Sinkiang-Tibet highway or Yehcheng-Gartok road in 1956 and the summer of 1957 with a view to opening up western Tibet to Chinese immigration and diverting its trade from its traditional southward direction northward into western China and the Soviet Union.

The attention of the Indian government was first drawn to this road by a very small-scale map published in a Chinese newspaper. To make sure whether the road had actually crossed through Indian territory, they decided to send two reconnaissance parties to Aksai Chin in the summer of 1958. One of these parties was arrested and kept in custody by the Chinese for at least five weeks. The other returned unmolested and submitted a report which showed that the new motor road "enters Indian territory just east of Sarigh Jilgnang, runs northwest to Amtogar and striking the western bank of the Amtogar lake runs northwest through Yangpa, Khitai Dawan and Haji Langar *which are all in indisputable Indian territory.*"[22]

Representations were then made to the government of China (in a note presented to the Chinese Ambassador in New Delhi on October 18, 1958) drawing their attention to this new encroachment on Indian territory and the arrest of fifteen members of the Indian reconnaissance party within Indian territorial limits. In their reply, dated November 1, 1958, the government of China, while informing the government of India of the release of Indian prisoners "in the spirit of Sino-Indian friendship," claimed that the region through which the Sinkiang-Tibet highway passed belonged entirely to them.[23] This was stated more categorically by Chou En-lai in his letter to Prime Minister Nehru dated January 23, 1959. The area of Ladakh, he said which India claimed as her territory, really belonged to the "southern part of China's Sinkiang-Uighur Autonomous Region, which has always been under Chinese jurisdiction. . . . And the Sinkiang-Tibet highway built by our country in 1956 runs through that area."[24] Possession is said to be nine points of the law. In Chinese eyes, it was the entire law, provided the disputed area was not in possession of the opposite party.

Parenthetically it may be stated here that Ladakh, which

originally belonged to Tibet, was conquered by Gulab Singh of Jammu, then a feudatory of the Sikhs, and annexed to his kingdom between 1832 and 1841. The annexation was confirmed by the conclusion of a treaty in 1842 between Maharaja Gulab Singh on one side and the Lama Guru Sahib of Lhasa and the representatives of the Chinese emperor on the other. This treaty mentioned the boundary between Ladakh and Tibet, but did not clearly demarcate it on the ground, obviously on the understanding that the boundary was well known.[25] When the British took over the suzerainty of Jammu and Kashmir state, they made repeated attempts to arrange a clear demarcation of the frontier. The Chinese government was asked to send its representatives for the purpose, but for one reason or another it did not. On January 13, 1847, however, the Chinese Amban wrote to the British government as follows: "I beg to observe that the borders of these territories have been sufficiently and distinctly fixed so that it would be best to adhere to this ancient arrangement, and it will prove far more convenient to abstain from any additional measures for fixing them." The British agreed to this suggestion, accepted the traditional boundary, and prepared their maps "on the basis of old usage and convention." "These maps," said Prime Minister Nehru in the Indian Parliament, "have been used in India for the last hundred years or so. They include the Aksai Chin region as part of Ladakh."[26]

It is noteworthy that Peking was silently pushing through the construction of this road through Indian territory, when Sino-Indian friendship was at its peak, when India was clamoring for the restitution of Formosa and offshore islands to the People's Government, when Chou En-lai was visiting India three times in the course of two months, repeatedly swearing by *Panch Shila* and proclaiming that: "The Chinese people deem it an honour to have such a great neighbour as India," and when the streets of Calcutta and Delhi swarmed with thronging crowds shouting *"Hindi Chini Bhai Bhai."*

It is equally noteworthy that neither the gradual shrinkage of India's traditional trade with Tibet, on which the livelihood of a section of her people depended, nor the continued publication of inflated Chinese maps, nor the growing Chinese intrusions into Indian territory were allowed to swerve India from her fixed policy of friendship toward China. In fact, the government of India kept back information regarding these intrusions from the Parliament and people of India lest it create any anti-Chinese feeling in the country. When asked in 1959 why he did not take the Parliament into his confidence regarding the construction of the Tibet-Sinkiang road through Aksai Chin, the Prime Minister stated that "the Government thought that it might progress by correspondence." In other words, he believed that the matter might be settled by negotiations and any kind of public clamor might do more harm than good.

In the meanwhile, the situation in Tibet had been steadily worsening. Discontent and unrest had been mounting, and revolts had broken out among the Goloks and Khambas in the eastern and northeastern borderlands. A resistance movement had been unmistakably gathering momentum.

Like all imperialists, the Chinese refused to see the mote in their own eye. They attributed this unrest to the "subversive and disruptive activities against China's Tibetan region carried out by the U. S. and the Chiang Kai-shek clique in collusion with fugitive reactionaries from Tibet" and local special agents, "using India's Kalimpong as a base;"[27] and they urged the government of India "to repress the subversive and disruptive activities against China's Tibetan region," and to deal sternly with certain persons whom they considered to be at the root of all troubles. In their reply, dated August 2, 1958, the government of India stated that they "have no evidence that the U. S. Government and the Kuomintang regime are using Kalimpong as a base for disruptive activities against China's Tibetan region;" that they have already warned some of the persons whom the Chinese Government had named, although there

was "no definite evidence that these persons have been in-
dulging in unlawful activities," and that they "will never permit any portion of its [India's] territory to be used as a base of
activities against any foreign Government, not to speak of the
friendly government of the People's Republic of China."[28]

To prevent annoyance to China, the government of India
also warned Tibetan officials resident in India not to make
statements on the Tibetan situation to newspaper correspondents. By and large, the Indian newspapers followed the government line and maintained a conspiracy of silence regarding
events and developments in Tibet. But what was withheld from
Indian newspapers could not be sealed off from the British
and European press. Mr. George N. Patterson, the correspondent of the *Daily Telegraph*, was therefore informed that unless
he "discontinued sending misleading and exaggerated messages
about Tibet to the *Daily Telegraph* or other foreign papers,
the Indian Government would be constrained to interdict his
residence in the districts of Darjeeling, Jalpaiguri and Cooch
Behar,"[29] The rapid development of events, however, soon revealed that Mr. Patterson was better informed about Tibet
than the government of India and his messages were not as
misleading and exaggerated as they were alleged to be.

chapter 6

REVOLT IN TIBET

IT IS ONE of the tragic ironies of history that China in spite of her long association with Tibet has never succeeded either in winning the allegiance of the Tibetans or in working out a durable understanding with them. The root of the trouble has always been Tibetan resentment against Han imperialism. Tibet is a nation in every sense of the word, and China's refusal to accept this patent fact has been the basic cause of the clashes and strife which have marked Sino-Tibetan relations for well-nigh two centuries.

Under the terms of the agreement of May, 1951, Communist China had undertaken to respect the internal "national regional autonomy" of Tibet. She had also promised not to "alter the established status, functions and powers of the Dalai Lama," "the religious beliefs, customs and habits of the Tibetan people," or "the income of the monasteries." The accord also provided that political, social, and economic reforms could be introduced in Tibet with the consent of the official Tibetan hierarchy upon the request of the people.

But the Chinese seem to have made these promises with all kinds of mental reservations. They had all the might and pride of a conquering race and the missionary zeal of a fanatical, revolutionary creed. They had no respect for either the Dalai Lama or the lamaist monasteries or the religious beliefs, customs, and habits of the Tibetan people. What they wanted was to secure a firm control over the strategic Tibetan plateau and to achieve its total integration into the highly centralized Chinese state. After an initial period of fraternization, therefore, they began to take one step after another which had the effect of nullifying the obligations they had undertaken under the terms of the agreement. This inevitably gave rise to resentment and resistance on the part of the Tibetan officialdom and people, resulting in clashes, "interrupted periodically by uneasy truces and compromises." This is the story in a nutshell of Sino-Tibetan relations in the years following 1951.

In the statements which the Dalai Lama issued from Tezpur on April 18, and from Mussoorie on June 20, 1959, he mentioned with great clarity and brevity some of the basic causes of the growing tension between Peking and Lhasa during these unhappy years. "It was . . . clear from the very beginning," he said at Mussoorie,

that the Chinese had no intentions of carrying out the agreement. Although they had solemnly undertaken to maintain my status and power as the Dalai Lama, they did not lose any opportunity to undermine my authority and sow dissension among my people. In fact, they compelled me, situated as I was, to dismiss my Prime Ministers under threat of their execution without trial, because they had in all honesty and sincerity resisted the unjustified usurpations of power by representatives of the Chinese Government in Tibet.

Far from carrying out the agreement they began deliberately to pursue a course of policy which was diametrically opposed to the terms and conditions which they had themselves laid down. Thus commenced a reign of terror which finds few parallels in the history of Tibet. Forced labour and compulsory exactions, a systematic persecution of the people, plunder and confiscations of property belonging to individuals and monasteries and execution of certain leading men in Tibet, these are the glorious achievements of Chinese rule in Tibet.

The Chinese, of course, do not admit the charges which have been leveled against them. Yet their official records contain statements which substantially corroborate the Tibetan version of the story. Thus on March 9, 1955, the Chinese government representative in Tibet reported as follows to Peking State Council:

Numerous are the shortcomings and errors on the part of the Chinese working personnel in Tibet. Part of the Han [Chinese] cadres have demonstrated a varying degree of the remnant concept of great Hanism, such as the lack of due respect to the religious beliefs, customs and habits of the Tibetans, the insufficient recognition of the merits of the Tibetan cadres, and the lack of due respect and warm support to them. . . .

Concerning the purchase and transport work, they fail to make timely price adjustments, causing part of the Tibetans a considerable loss for which compensation and amends have to be made later. In individual cases, there has even been breach of law and discipline and phenomenon of commandism.

Again in October, 1957, Fan Ming, member of the Chinese Communist Tibetan Work Committee, reported:

Great-Han chauvinism in Tibet is manifested in the feeling of superiority of the Han race, repugnance at the backwardness of Tibet, discrimination against Tibet, distortion of Tibet, failure to respect the freedom of religious belief and traditional customs of the Tibetan people. . . . As a result, some cases have occurred where the nationalities policy was impaired, law and discipline were violated and the freedom of religious belief and customs of the Tibetans were not respected.

Any detailed examination of the causes of the Tibetan revolt of 1959 does not fall within the scope of this book. But a few essential facts may be stated with a view to dispelling certain misconceptions which the Chinese Communists and their admirers in other countries have sought to create. The revolt was not an uprising of "the reactionary clique of the upper strata," aided and abetted by "imperialists" and "foreign reactionaries," as the Chinese stated. Nor was it a struggle between the forces of reaction and those of progress or between traditionalism and Communism, as some others have asserted. In the ultimate analysis, it was an assertion of Tibetan nationalism against Chinese imperialism, or as Prime Minister Nehru stated in the Indian Parliament, "a nationalist upsurge." It sprang fundamentally from the basic incompatibility between Chinese eagerness to wipe out the last remnants of Tibetan autonomy and the Tibetan attempt to preserve that autonomy and the distinctive Tibetan way of life.

By common consent the Dalai Lama was the symbol of Tibetan nationalism. He was the God-king of the Tibetan people, respected and revered as no earthly potentate is respected and revered anywhere else in the world. It therefore became an objective of Chinese policy to secularize the personality of the Dalai Lama and bring him out into the open, so as to make it possible for the Tibetans to see that there was nothing extraordinary about the man whom they had for centuries regarded as the reincarnation of the bodhisattva Chenre-si (Avalokiteshwara), the embodiment of compassion and benevolence. The Dalai Lama's authority in Tibet depended in a large measure upon the prestige of his personality. If by some device he could be robbed of that prestige, the Chinese game in Tibet would be easily won. But the Chinese failed to rob the Dalai Lama of either his traditional prestige or the love and respect of his people. They therefore hit upon the plan of making him a willing tool in their hands. In spite of the strong opposition of the Tibetan people, they took him to Peking for one year on the plea of his participation in the Chinese People's Congress, and subjected him to a kind of indoctrination. But the Dalai Lama survived the indoctrination and did not become a Chinese tool.

Alongside these measures, the Chinese also took various steps to reduce his powers and circumscribe his jurisdiction. They divided Tibet into three administrative zones, in two of which anti-Lhasa elements were put in power. One of these was the Chamdo area, where the People's Liberation Army had first penetrated in their invasion of Tibet. This area was taken out of the jurisdiction of the Lhasa government and handed over to a People's Liberation Committee, which set up its own organs of administration, manned either by the Chinese or by pronouncedly pro-Chinese Tibetans. The area round about Shigatse and covering the populous sections of the province of Tsang was similarly placed under the administrative control of the Panchen Lama, who, installed some years ago by the Chinese Nationalists at Kumbum outside Tibet, now returned to Tashilunpo in the baggage of the victors to play the role of a Tibetan anti-Pope.[1] Here also the pro-Chinese and anti-Lhasa elements were given the upper hand; and Peking steadily pursued the policy of building up the stature of the Panchen Lama so as to present him to the Tibetan masses at least as the Dalai Lama's equal. In Lhasa itself the Chinese tried various insidious tactics to reduce the powers of the Dalai Lama. In 1953-54 they made an attempt to supplant the Tibetan local government by a Political and Military Committee, but owing to the bitter opposition of the Tibetan people the idea was dropped.

On March 9, 1955, a Preparatory Committee for the Formation of a Tibetan Autonomous Region was set up by a resolution of the Chinese State Council. (The Committee was not, however, officially installed till April 22, 1956.) It was designed to be the sole agency of administration for the whole of Tibet "with a decisive voice in every significant sector of the region's social, political and economic life."[2] The Dalai Lama was appointed Chairman with Panchen Ngoertehni and General

Chang Kuo-hua as his deputies and the collaborationist Kaloon Ngabo (Ngabo Ngawang Jigme) as the Secretary-General. But the composition of the Committee was so designed as to ensure Peking's absolute majority. Thus when the Committee was finally formed, it came to consist of ten representatives of Tibet local government (Dalai Lama's government), ten from the Panchen Kanpo Lija (Panchen Lama's court), ten from the National Liberation Committee of the Chamdo Area (thus putting the Dalai Lama's government on a footing of equality with the two spurious rival governments set up by the Chinese), five from among the Central People's Government personnel in Tibet, and seventeen from religious and popular organizations. As the representatives of the Panchen Kanpo Lija, Chamdo Area, the Central People's Government and of some of the so-called popular organizations were all nominees of Peking, Peking had an absolute majority in the committee. To make matters doubly certain, the committee was made directly subordinate to the Chinese State Council and all its decisions had to be confirmed by the latter. The autonomy of Tibet was thus reduced to a mere mockery.

Simultaneously with these onslaughts on Tibetan autonomy, the Chinese Communists embarked upon a twofold program of large-scale indoctrination and of vilification of Tibetan monks, monasteries, and the Buddhist religion. No sooner was the Chinese Military Area Headquarters set up in Tibet in 1952 than it opened a "Cultural Department" to indoctrinate the Tibetans in Marxist philosophy. Before long various Communist and Communist-front organizations were opened to carry on the campaign under various subterfuges. To name a few, a Tibetan Department of the New Democratic Youth Federation of China was founded on May 4, 1952, an Association of the Patriotic Youth of Tibet was founded on February 13, 1953, and a Women's Patriotic Federation was founded on March 8, 1954. These operated, and were meant to operate, side by side with the numerous branches of the Chinese Communist Party, opened in various areas of Tibet soon after "liberation."

The Chinese, no doubt, worked hard to spread education among the people. They opened a large number of schools in Lhasa and other parts of Tibet, but the education which was imparted through these schools was entirely divorced from Tibetan traditions and based upon a Communist-oriented curriculum.

As if these measures were not enough, a systematic campaign of calumny was carried on against the religious beliefs of the people in the Communist-controlled Tibetan language newspapers. Monks were held up as swindlers and exploiters, monasteries as nests of ignorance and reaction, and gods as a "false invention for deceiving people." Even the great Buddha was not spared. An authorized version of his life on approved Communist principles was prepared and put in circulation:

The founder of Buddhism was Sakya Muni. . . . His kingdom was very aggressive among all the Indian kingdoms of his time. It always used to invade the small kingdoms. It was during the reign of Sakya Muni that his subjects revolted against him and later other small kingdoms also rose against him simultaneously. As they attacked Sakya Muni, he accepted defeat and escaped amidst the fighting. Since there was no other way out for him, he wandered into the forests. Having founded Buddhism, he brought about pessimism and idleness in the minds of the people weakening their courage and thus reached his goal of re-domination over them. This fact was clearly recorded in history.[3]

Moreover, in spite of the undertaking the Chinese had given to protect the monasteries and desist from effecting any change in their incomes, they sometimes robbed the monasteries of their stocks of grain, imposed heavy taxes upon them, and compelled the monks to work in the fields and on roads. As the Tibetan resistance movement grew, old and venerable monasteries were bombed and destroyed and unspeakable atrocities were committed upon incarnate lamas held in respect among the people.

"We have evidence of instances and cases," says the report of the International Commission of Jurists, "where the heads of monasteries have been killed, imprisoned and publicly humiliated. One case in our file refers to a very highly respected Lama who was stripped and dragged with rope over a rocky terrain, as a result of which he died." "In the province of Kham alone," the report adds, "250 monasteries were destroyed. Cases have been reported of Head Lamas being dragged to death by horses, and a fairly large number sent as prisoners to concentration camps in China."[4]

Soon after their occupation of Tibet, the Chinese began to show a kind of feverish zeal for the construction of roads and highways in the country. "The labour for this work was Tibetan men, women and children, laymen and monks, many of them forcibly drafted for the work. It is alleged that up to 200,000 were forced into these labour projects and about one-fourth of them are said to have died from the cold weather, hunger and fatigue." The *World Jurists'* Report quotes a witness as saying: "The financial and physical losses sustained goes into thousands of acres of agricultural land. The Chinese destroyed agricultural lands, irrigation systems and ancient consolidated holdings by indiscriminately using the tracts in the name of highway priority. Numerous religious monuments, shrines, Maniwalls and even houses of poor peasants that were in the path of the highway or road were destroyed."[5]

The economic impact of "liberation" was also not altogether happy. True, Peking prevailed on the local administration to take some decisive steps toward alleviating the oppressive financial burdens on the lower classes and lessening the economic dependence of the peasants and cattle-raisers on the whims of the nobility, monasteries and landowners. "Taxes were lowered, the permitted interest rate on loans was reduced and the Government prohibited the seizure of mortgaged peasant land-holdings for non-payment of debts, those already forfeited being ordered to be returned to the owners."[6] Moreover, a hydroelectric station, leatherworks and ironworks were set up at Lhasa, dikes were repaired and built elsewhere, and dams were constructed to protect Lhasa and Shigatse from floods. On the other hand, the monopolization of Tibetan foreign trade by a joint Sino-Tibetan Syndicate (which was really a Chinese syndicate) and the handling of all sales of Tibetan products through a Peking-operated General Tibetan Commercial Corporation led to considerable bitterness and dislocation among traditional Tibetan trading classes. But what seems to have produced almost intolerable confusion and distress was the large-scale influx of Chinese immigrants into Tibet, not merely in the shape of troops and officials and party cadres, but as settlers in the eastern and north eastern borderlands of the country.

Peking appears to have formed the grand design of Sinicizing Tibet by bringing millions and millions of Chinese colonists into the country. At the historic meeting on September 20, 1955, between Mao Tse-tung, the Dalai Lama, and Panchen Rampoche, Mao had indicated that, among the impending changes, Communist China intended to colonize Tibet at a ratio of more than five to one. On April 26, 1956, General Chang Kuo-hua, quoting Mao, stated: "Tibet is a huge area but thinly populated. Efforts must be made to raise the population from the present level of two millions . . . to more than ten millions." In fact, large-scale settlement of the Chinese began from 1955 onward in the Golak and Amdo areas of eastern Tibet; and the unsettlement which it produced among the native population, half peasants and half nomads, coupled with the highhandedness of the Chinese troops detailed to protect Chinese interests, led to the first post-"liberation" armed revolts in Tibet at the end of 1955 and beginning of 1956.

Elsewhere too the presence of this huge Chinese population proved to be a great burden on Tibetan economy. "Before the advent of the Chinese," stated Thubten Nyenjik, former abbot of Gyangtse monastery, who was also governor of Gyangtse province,

the economy of Tibet was sound, the cost of living low, and the Tibetan Government was in a position to aid its people in their economic, social, cultural and spiritual aspirations. But now, owing to the influx of one hundred thousand Chinese soldiers who live off the Tibetans, their granaries were empty, for the Chinese take 'loans' which are never repaid; the vast herds of yaks and flocks of sheep have been decimated; trees in Government and private owned parks up-rooted for firewood; and the economy of the country so disrupted that the cost of living for the bare necessities of life have risen nine to ten times, and where formerly there was a large exportable surplus, these have now to be imported.

"The Chinese have built roads," Thubten Nyenjik added, "but these are military roads, indispensable for holding down a conquered people and built with the help of forced Tibetan labour and the 'loan' of vast quantities of grain and silver from the reserve granaries and treasury of the Government of Tibet."

It was stated by another Tibetan refugee,[7] that when the Chinese immigrants poured into Tibet, they "brought nothing with them but their mugs and their chopsticks," and the effect of their inroads on essential supplies was to make prices rise five or six times.

When the ensuing economic distress led to a popular outcry, the Chinese replied with the assurance that after the motor roads from China were completed, prices would return to the normal level. This reason was invoked to justify the exaction of 'voluntary' labour to build roads, the road gangs receiving no wages and providing even their own rations. But when the first vehicles began to arrive in 1953 they brought not more supplies but more and more Chinese. Prices rose still further.

In fact, food prices shot up as much as thirty times the previous prices, because of the influx of Chinese personnel.[8]

These, then, were some of the causes fomenting unrest and opposition against the Chinese in Tibet. As early as 1952 there emerged an anti-Communist secret "people's committee," and in 1953 the first Tibetan national party. Gradually opposition turned into hostility, resulting in open revolts. It was in the eastern provinces, where the Chinese pressure was the greatest, that the first uprisings took place at the end of 1955 and the beginning of 1956 among the Golaks and the Amdos. Then they spread to other areas, particularly among the Khampa tribes, traditionally opposed to any outside political authority. The Chinese resorted to methods of fire and sword to suppress the rebels. "Everywhere there were scenes of slaughter and promiscuous butchery. . . . Monasteries, towns, heaps of human corpses and ruined fields presented a picture of chaos and bleak gloom."[9] The Khampas resorted to guerrilla tactics, trapped the Chinese contingents in numerous ambushes, destroyed and burned their vehicles and sometimes took away their arms. And gradually the conflagration spread, from east to west, till in March, 1959, Lhasa itself was engulfed.

That Tibet was heading toward a crisis was not unknown in India in spite of the bamboo curtain. At the time of the coronation of King Mahendra of Nepal (May 2, 1956) rumors of disturbances on the Roof of the World were widely talked about at Katmandu. Toward the end of the same year (November 25, 1956), when the Dalai Lama came to India in connection with the celebration of the twenty-fifth centenary of the *mahaparinirvana* of Lord Buddha, he was already so upset about the situation in Tibet that at one moment he decided not to go back to Lhasa. This he revealed in his Mussoorie statement (June 20, 1959).

As I was unable to do anything for the benefit of my people, [he said] I had practically made up my mind when I came to India not to return to Tibet until there was a manifest change in the attitude of the Chinese authorities. I, therefore, sought the advice of the Prime Minister of India who has always shown me unfailing kindness and consideration. After his talk with the Chinese Prime Minister and on the strength of the assurances given by him on behalf of China, Mr. Nehru advised me to change my decision.

While in India the Dalai Lama, obviously with the concurrence of Peking, had invited Nehru to pay a visit to Lhasa to see the situation in Tibet for himself. The Prime Minister accordingly planned to proceed to Lhasa and Bhutan in September, 1958. But before he actually undertook the journey, he was curtly told by China that the invitation extended to him earlier was withdrawn. No reasons were given; but it seemed clear that things were not all right in Tibet and Peking did not want Nehru to see them for himself. It was, however, immediately announced from New Delhi that in spite of the cancellation of his visit to Lhasa, the Prime Minister would proceed to Bhutan according to schedule. And he did proceed to Bhutan, passing through fifteen miles of Tibetan territory, thus reaffirming India's interest in the maintenance of Bhutan's independence. In the first week of March, 1959, the Prime Minister of Bhutan paid a visit to New Delhi and confirmed the existence of unsettled conditions in Tibet.

The news of the flare-up in Lhasa, therefore, came as no surprise to India. Yet at the outset there was hardly any realization of the extent and character of the upheaval. But as news flowed in and the magnitude of the tragedy was realized, there was an outburst of public feeling in the country the like of which was seldom witnessed on any other international issue. Even Prime Minister Nehru, always cautious in his statements concerning Communist countries, confessed that events in Tibet "affected some deeper chords in Indian hearts."

The sequence of events in Lhasa was briefly as follows. Since March 10, following a rumor that the Chinese planned to kidnap the Dalai Lama, there had been large-scale demonstrations in the city. The entire Lhasa proletariat, along with the monks and Khampas, were on the streets, tearing off anti-Western posters from the walls, putting up anti-Communist posters in their place, and shouting anti-Chinese slogans. Crowds of demonstrators numbering ten thousand or more went to the Indian, Nepalese, and Bhutanese consulates and spoke about their grievances and apprehensions. There were also big demonstrations by women, headed by members of the Communist-inspired Patriotic Women's Association and wives of leading

Tibetan officials. About 5,000 of them went to be Indian consulate and requested the Consul-General to accompany them
to the Chinese Foreign Bureau and be a witness to their presenting certain demands. As was natural in such circumstances,
the Consul-General pleaded his inability to accede to their
request. Meanwhile, thousands of Tibetans, men and women,
surrounded the Norbulinka, the summer palace where the
Dalai Lama was staying, so as to ensure that no Chinese came
near their God-king. On March 17 the Chinese garrison in
Lhasa fired a few shells which fell into the palace courtyard.
That day the decision was taken that the Dalai Lama must flee
from Tibet and seek asylum in India. At night, dressed in
ordinary lama clothes, he slipped out of the palace and began
his hazardous trek across the mountains.

On March 14 fierce fighting broke out in the city. But it was
an unequal battle from beginning to end, and "in two days of
merciless fighting the Chinese killed thousands of Tibetans. No
figures are available but more than ten thousand Lhasa Tibetans are known to have disappeared, either killed or sent into
forced labour in other parts."

"The two hundred members of the Dalai Lama's bodyguard
who had been left behind were disarmed, then publicly
machine-gunned. The famous three monasteries of Sera, Drepung and Ganden were shelled, and Sera and Drepung dam-
aged beyond repair, priceless manuscripts and treasures being
destroyed. Thousands of monks from these monasteries were
either killed on the spot, made to work in the city as slaves, or
deported to other parts."[10]

News of these grave incidents in Tibet was received by the
government of India with great caution and released with
greater restraint. On March 6 Prime Minister Nehru, asked by
pressmen to comment upon reports from Tibet, said that it
was well known that there had been troubles in certain parts of
Tibet connected with people who were called Khampas; but
he could not say anything about the extent of these troubles.

He, however, cautioned them against being taken in by exaggerated reports in the press. "I cannot tell you to what extent
trouble exists in some parts of Tibet, but often the news that
appears in the press about Tibet is grossly exaggerated, for the
simple reason that the persons who give that news are refugees
who seldom are accurate witnesses of anything. They are
partisans who believe every rumour."[11] On March 17, the day
on which the Dalai Lama fled from Lhasa, the Prime Minister
in the course of a review of the international situation in the
Parliament briefly referred to the difficulties in Tibet. "But it
is," he said, "more a clash of wills at present than a clash of
arms or physical bodies."

On March 20, however, a news release issued from New
Delhi stated that widespread rebellion had broken out in Tibet,
in which the Tibetans and the Khampas were fighting the
Chinese in Lhasa and the countryside. On March 23 the Prime
Minister again made a statement in the Lok Sabha in which he
revealed that the Indian consulate building at Lhasa had been
hit by bullets in consequence of firing in the neighborhood and
that the Chinese had ordered the consulate staff to stay inside
the consulate until further notice. He also expressed his anxiety
for the safety of the Dalai Lama but hastened to add that
"India had no intention of interfering in the internal affairs of
China, with whom we have friendly relations." There were
angry scenes in the House on that day. Leaders of most opposition groups in Parliament (except the Communists) asked the
Speaker to allow discussion of the Tibetan situation and the
question of granting asylum to Tibetan refugees. An adjournment motion was tabled by Mr. N. G. Goray (leader of the
Praja Socialist Party). But these were all ruled out on the
ground that "discussion on the internal affairs of another
country had never been allowed in this House."[12]

There was nevertheless widespread expression of sympathy
for Tibet outside the Parliament. On March 27 a committee for
solidarity with the people of Tibet was formed at Bombay. On
March 29 a "Tibet Day" was observed in New Delhi. On March

30 "Hands off Tibet" demonstrations were held before the Chinese Embassy at New Delhi and the Chinese consulate in Calcutta. Demands were also made from certain quarters that the government of India should take the Tibet issue to the United Nations.

On March 28 the Chinese State Council formally dissolved the Tibetan Local Government, made the puppet Panchen Lama the Chairman of the Preparatory Committee, and replaced some of its other members by collaborationists. At the same time a communiqué was issued through the *Hsinhua* (Chinese official news agency), giving the Chinese version of Tibetan developments. The rebellion in Tibet was described as an uprising of "the reactionary clique of the upper strata," representing "imperialism and the most reactionary big serf owners." It was "engineered by the imperialists, the Chiang Kai-shek bandits and foreign reactionaries; the commanding centre of the rebellion was in Kalimpong." The communiqué further stated that whereas the Chinese policy in Tibet was "based on unity, equality and gradual realisation of regional national autonomy," the rebels wanted the "so called independence of Tibet" and raised such "reactionary" slogans as "Drive out the Han people" and "Independence for Tibet." The communiqué also referred to the discussion of Tibetan affairs in the Indian Parliament and stated that China "considers such discussion of the internal affairs of a friendly country to be impolite and improper."

The fat was now fairly on the fire. The Chinese communiqué led to an immediate storm of protest, no less in the Parliament than in the press. The Prime Minister again spoke in the Parliament on March 30. "It is wrong to say," he categorically stated, "that Kalimpong was the centre from which anti-Chinese activities were directed. . . . to imagine or to say a small group of persons sitting in Kalimpong organised a major upheaval in Tibet seems to me to make a large draft on imagination and to slur over obvious facts." He also upheld the rights of the Indian Parliament to discuss any matter it chose. The Indian

Parliament, he said, "is not going to be limited in the exercise of its rights of discussion by any external or internal authority, wherever it may be." On the Tibet-China question also he gave the country an inkling of his mind. Although "it is important for us to have friendly relations with the great country, China," he stated, "our sympathies are with the Tibetans. We want them to progress in freedom."

This was a historic statement. Restrained and dignified, it showed where India stood in relation to China and Tibet. It marked the beginning of the end of the Sino-Indian honeymoon. The Chinese, who had almost taken Jawaharlal Nehru for granted, discovered that he was much too big for Mao's pocket, and that however anxious he might be to seek the friendship of China, he would not seek it at the cost of India's honor and dignity.

The Communist Party of India, which had consistently echoed the Chinese line and given all-out support to Chinese policy in Tibet and even to Chinese charges against India, came in for considerable castigation in and outside the Parliament. Speaking in the Lok Sabha on April 5, the Prime Minister said: ". . . the Communist Party has uprooted itself from these matters (which are so deeply rooted in national sentiment that they override even party boundaries) and feels quite differently. I am not talking about politics or economics but of what is called national sentiment which has deep roots in the country. We saw there [in the Lok Sabha] that marked distinction of people, who, however, they differ among themselves, had a common bond, a strong national tradition and sentiment." But the Indian Communists, he stated, seemed to have no kinship with this national sentiment.

On March 31 the Dalai Lama, fleeing from Chinese fury, marching day and night through difficult mountains and rivers but shielded by the loyalty of his people and the heroism of the Khampa tribesmen, crossed the Indian frontier at Towang in the Kameng Division of the North-East Frontier Agency. He and his entourage were given political asylum by the government of India. The New China News Agency immediately reported that the Dalai Lama had entered India "under duress." It was later insinuated that he had been kidnapped into India by "Indian expansionists." When the Dalai Lama issued his first statement to the press at Tezpur on April 18, denying that he had been kidnapped or that he was under duress in India and exposing China's consistent record of double-dealing and perfidy in Tibet, the New China News Agency reported (April 20, 1959) that the statement was issued under duress and that foreign (meaning Indian) elements had helped to shape it. "One has reason to believe," it stated, "that the statement was not by the Dalai Lama but was imposed on him by some person or persons." On April 22, the Panchen Lama, speaking before the National People's Congress at Peking, asserted that "the so-called statement" by the Dalai Lama "was imposed on him by foreigners."

On the same day (April 22) the Dalai Lama issued a second statement from Mussoorie, in course of which he said: "I wish to make it clear that the earlier statement was issued under my authority and indicated my view and I stand by it." But the Chinese press again insinuated that this statement, like the earlier one, was drafted by the officers of the government of India and issued under duress.

In the meanwhile, deputies of China's National People's Congress, meeting at Peking, went on, day in and day out, condemning "Indian imperialists for scheming the Tibetan rebellion and interfering in China's internal affairs with the intention to split Tibet from China." One Chinese deputy, described as an expert on international law, stated: "The backing and encouragement certain Indian politicians gave the rebellious clique in Tibet and the issuing of the so-called statement which was imposed on the Dalai Lama constitute a barbarous act of interference. . . . We [the Chinese] will never allow foolish hogs to poke their snouts into our beautiful garden." The puppet Panchen Lama went a step further and ascribed all the sufferings of Tibet, past and present, to "the vicious machination of the British aggressors and their running dogs." "It is worth noting," he added, "that the reactionaries in India, working in the footsteps of the British imperialists, have always harboured expanionist ambitions towards Tibet and have carried out various forms of sabotage activities which are undoubtedly favourable to imperialism and unfavourable to Sino-Indian friendship." Another, Deputy Li Chi-shen, asked: "If their [Tibetan] rebellion has no connections with Indian expanionists, why are certain Indian political figures so sympathetic with the traitorous crimes of the Tibetan reactionary clique? . . . Why is it that the so-called 'Dalai Lama's statement' was distributed by an Indian diplomatic official?" "The ambitions of these expansionists," he added, "are really not small. They practically want to turn Tibet into their colony or protectorate."[13]

Warnings and threats to India were also not wanting. On April 24 the *People's Daily* proclaimed in a banner headline over eight columns in black Chinese characters, half an inch high: "Deputies of various nationalists give solemn warnings to Indian expansionists." On April 25 the Peking radio solemnly warned: "British imperialists and Indian expansionists had better clarify their minds or they will suffer a tragic end." On April 30 the *People's Daily* held out the threat: "We give solemn warning to imperialists and Indian expansionists. You must stop at once; otherwise you will be crushed to pieces under the iron fist of 650 million Chinese people."

Stunned by this ceaseless torrent of abuse, slander, and intimidation, Prime Minister Nehru again made a statement on the Tibet question in the Lok Sabha on April 27. Regarding the Chinese calumnies and charges, he said: "All I can say is that I have been greatly distressed at the tone of the comments and the charges made against India by respectable people in China. They have used the language of the cold war regardless of truth and propriety." He described the charges as "unbecoming," "fantastic," and "entirely devoid of substance." He also reviewed the whole Tibet issue once again, explained what he thought to be the genesis of the recent troubles, and reiterated what he had stated earlier regarding the Indian attitude to the problem. "We have no desire whatever to interfere in Tibet," he repeated. "We have every desire to maintain the friendship between India and China: but at the same time we have every sympathy for the people of Tibet and we are greatly distressed at their hapless plight. We hope still that the authorities of China in their wisdom will not use their great strength against the Tibetans but will win them to friendly cooperation in accordance with the assurances they have themselves given about the autonomy of Tibet region."

"What have we done about this matter of Tibet," asked the Prime Minister, speaking in the Rajya Sabha on May 4, "apart from speeches and odd things? India had received the Dalai Lama and a few thousand refugees giving them asylum. Is it suggested that we should have refused to give asylum to the Dalai Lama when he asked for it? If it is suggested by someone outside India, I can tell him that—I do not know about all—out of 400 million people I doubt if even a few thousands would have agreed with our policy. Hundreds and millions of Indians would have become angry at that action of ours if we had refused asylum to the Dalai Lama and his party. It was an impossible policy and utterly wrong thing for us to do—political, humanitarian, anyway you like."[14]

About a month earlier (April 5), Nehru had stated at a press conference in New Delhi that the Indian attitude concerning the question of Tibet was governed by three factors: (1) preservation of the security and integrity of India, (2) India's desire to maintain friendly relations with China, and (3) India's deep sympathy for the people of Tibet. This was the first time that the Prime Minister openly hinted that Indian security was involved in the problem of Tibet. All these years never perhaps wholly absent from his mind (see chapter 3 and 4), it was also never uppermost in his mind. In any case, he thought he would be able to ensure Indian security by cultivating the friendship of Communist China. But Tibet upset his calculations. With the destruction of Tibetan autonomy and the placing of Tibet under a huge Chinese army of occupation, what had been implicit since 1950 became explicit.

Nehru apparently saw the danger more clearly now than ever before. Fresh measures were therefore undertaken to strengthen India's border security. Nepal, Bhutan, and Sikkim joined with India in coordinating border security measures, although each country still had its own pattern of frontier patrols. The territory of the NEFA was closed to all except those of the NEFA administration, and patrolling of the frontier and watching of the check-posts by crack Assam rifles was intensified.[15] This does not mean that Nehru had yet lost all faith in Peking. He still hoped and believed in the possibility of a rapprochement between the Chinese and the Dalai Lama on the basis of Tibetan autonomy.[16] In any case, he was clearly of the opinion that India's friendly relations with China must be maintained.

On May 16, 1959, the Chinese Ambassador in New Delhi met the Foreign Secretary in the External Affairs Ministry and made a bitter and impolite statement regarding Nehru's attitude toward Tibet, his attribution of the Tibetan revolt to "a strong feeling of nationalism," his refusal to accept the Chinese version of the story, his defense of the "freedom of speech" of the Indian Parliament, and above all "the impressive welcome extended to the Dalai Lama by the Indian Government." The Chinese Ambassador continued:

The enemy of the Chinese people lies in the East—the U.S. imperialists have many military bases in Taiwan, in South Korea, Japan and in the Philippines which are all directed against China. China's main attention and policy of struggle are directed to the east, to the west Pacific region, to the vicious and aggressive U.S. imperialism, and not to India or any other country in the South East Asia and South Asia. Although the Philippines, Thailand

and Pakistan have joined the SEATO which is designed to oppose China, we have not treated those countries as our principal enemy; our principal enemy is U.S. imperialism. . . . China will not be so foolish as to antagonise the United States in the east and again antagonise India in the west. . . . We cannot have two centres of attention, nor can we take friend for foe. . . . Friends! It seems to us that you cannot have two fronts. Is it not so? If it is, here then lies the meeting point of our two sides.[17]

What a staggering revelation of the Chinese motives behind Sino-Indian friendship and Peking's loud protestations of love for the *Panch Shila!* There could no longer be any doubt that the existence of United States bases in the western Pacific zone was the *raison d'être* behind China's make-believe adherence to the principles of peaceful coexistence with India and other Southeast Asian countries. Once these bases were liquidated or withdrawn, the *raison d'être* for friendship would also disappear. Yet for almost a decade India has been crying for the liquidation of United States bases in East Asia and the return of Formosa and the offshore islands to Communist China. The danger which she wanted to avoid by cultivating the friendship of Peking would have been precipitated if her pleadings had been listened to by the White House.

To the statement of the Chinese Ambassador, the government of India's reply was short. It expressed regret and surprise that the Chinese statement "is not only not in consonance with certain facts, but is also wholly out of keeping with diplomatic usage and the courtesies due to friendly countries." Regarding Peking's attitude toward *Panch Shila* or the five principles of peaceful existence, the Indian note said: "This is an approach with which the Government of India are not in agreement. They have proclaimed and adhered to these principles as matters of basic policy and not of opportunism. They will continue to hold to these principles and endeavour to apply them according to their own thinking."[18]

chapter 7

CHINESE INTRUSIONS AND CLAIMS

THE TRAGEDY of Tibet cast a deep shadow upon Sino-Indian relations. It undermined India's faith in Chinese *bona fides*. On the other hand, it infuriated the Chinese against the people and government of India. For Prime Minister Nehru it was at once a shock and a disillusionment. He saw the fabric of Sino-Indian friendship, which he had sought all these years to build up with such infinite care and patience, crumbling to pieces. He saw one of the major planks of his foreign policy collapsing before his eyes. Inevitably he was perturbed. "It is a deeper tragedy for many of us," he said with profound regret, "even than the events in Tibet that something we have laboured for, in the Five Principles and at Bandung, should have suffered in people's minds and become depreciated."[1] But he decided to salvage what he could from the wreck.

For the Tibetans he had profound and limitless sympathy. But he would not allow that sympathy to come in the way of his friendship with China. He still seems to have believed that the Chinese would see the error of their ways and seek to bring about a rapprochement with the Dalai Lama on the basis of Tibetan autonomy. "I cannot imagine any feasible, practical or happy solution without the autonomy of the Tibetan people," he said at Madras on April 14. "We accept Chinese overlordship, but I do earnestly hope that the Tibetan people will maintain and be able to enjoy their autonomy and not be oppressed and suppressed by others and that sooner or later some such settlement will be arrived at."[2] In his view, guarded expression of opinions and sympathies in India would not only pave the path for such a settlement but would go a long way toward restoring India's friendship with China. On April 6 he declared at Allahabad that although India had full sympathy with the Tibetans, she must not take any action which would "in any way affect the 2,000-year-old friendship between India and China." On April 10, addressing the Parliamentary Consultative Committee on Foreign Affairs, he stressed the vital need of preventing the cold war atmosphere from pervading India in the wake of the happenings in Tibet. On April 24 he reiterated at Mussoorie that India's interest in Tibet was "historical, sentimental and religious, and not essentially political." On May 9 he urged the Congress Working Committee to observe restraint whenever they spoke on Tibet and "expressed his keen desire to maintain friendly relations with China." The Working Committee accordingly adopted a resolution expressing its anxiety "that there should be friendly relations with China." Nehru also discouraged the expression of organized public sympathy for Tibet; and when a Tibet Convention was planned in Calcutta, he indirectly asked members of the Congress Party not to associate themselves with it.

The Dalai Lama had been granted political asylum in India, but he was informed that he was not expected "to function on the political plane," and in making statements he should see to it that India's relations with China were not compromised. In a news conference at Mussoorie (June 20, 1959), the Dalai Lama had stated: "Wherever I am, accompanied by my Government, the Tibetan people recognised us as the Government by law." Immediately the Government of India came out with a counterblast, repudiating the claim of the Dalai Lama and refusing him the status of an *émigré* government. "The Government of India want to make to make it clear," the statement ran, "that they do not recognise any separate government of Tibet and there is, therefore, no question of a Tibetan government under the Dalai Lama functioning in India".[3] Restrictions were also imposed on foreign journalists in the matter of communicating with Tibetan refugees except through official interpreters, in the belief that critical or derogatory statements regarding Chinese rule in Tibet emanating from northern India might further strain India-China relations. New Delhi, moreover, made it known early in July, 1959, that despite all that had happened in Tibet and Peking's general cynical attitude toward international obligations, India would repeat her initiative of the last two years toward replacing Formosa by Peking in the China seat in the Security Council. Desperately Nehru followed a course of restraint and caution, apparently hoping that it would evoke some sort of sympathetic response in Peking's Red oligarchy.

The Red oligarchy, however, was in a different mood. True, there was a temporary abatement of the orgy of anti-Indian vituperation in China. But the taps shut in Peking were opened with almost equal vehemence in Lhasa. Here the Chinese launched upon an insidious, anti-Indian propaganda through Tibetan-language newspapers, broadsheets, and bulletins, telling the Tibetans that Indians were exploiters who had inherited all the traditions of British imperialism. In the Goebellian style false stories were manufactured and circulated regarding the "evil deeds" of Indian physicians and of the former Indian military escort in Tibet before they were eliminated by the agreement of 1954.[4] At the same time the Chinese officers in Tibet went about proclaiming that they would before long "liberate" Sikkim, Bhutan, Ladakh, and NEFA, which were being wrongfully held by the "Indian imperialists."[5] Vital border areas were similarly saturated with propaganda and people were told that if Tibet was the palm of China's hand, Bhutan, NEFA, Sikkim, Nepal, and Ladakh were its fingers. Presumably now that the palm was restored to China, the fingers must go with it.[6]

Moreover, without openly repudiating the agreement of 1954, Peking now began to put serious obstacles in the way of the functioning of Indian consulates and trade posts and of Indian pilgrims and traders in Tibet, presumably with a view to wiping out the last traces of Indian connection with that country. The Indian Trade Agency buildings at Gyangtse had been washed away by floods. After prolonged negotiations, it had been decided to begin the construction of a new building in May, 1959. Peking was, therefore, requested "that the local authorities may be instructed to give help in procuring timber, stones and bricks and in making available the necessary transport for construction work." But the local authorities, instead of extending cooperation, created "all manner of difficulties" in the way of construction. Laborers were ordered "under threat of arrest" to stop working on the site. Owners of horse carts were instructed not to lift bricks to the Trade Agency site. Dealers who supplied *arca* (mortar) were prohibited from making deliveries to the Agency.[7] Similar obstacles were created in the way of maintenance and repairs of other Trade Agencies. Moreover, Indian officials in the consulate-general at Lhasa and other centers were closely watched and subjected to various disabilities in the pursuit of their normal official functions. So were Indian traders and pilgrims. They were not permitted to visit even recognised marts at Phari and Gyangtse, much less Shigatse and Lhasa. They could not travel freely nor could they get transport to send their goods from one place to another. Finally, to completely paralyze Indian traders, the currency regulations of Tibet were suddenly changed (July, 1959), making the use of Indian currency illegal and fixing the exchange value of Tibetan currency at 25 per cent of its previous value. Indian traders found their stocks depreciated by 75 per cent overnight. On August 6, 1959, Prime Minister Nehru told the Indian Parliament that India's trade with Tibet had undergone a sharp decline. In February India's import trade with Tibet amounted to Rs. 1,500,000 and export to Rs. 1,000,-000. By June the figures came down to Rs. 200,000 and Rs. 300,000 respectively.

Alongside these anti-Indian maneuvers, Peking now kicked up a row over another issue. Several hundred Ladakhis, lamas and Muslims, had been resident in Tibet for years either for trade or for study. Some had been there for two or three generations. But they did not hold any travel papers or identity certificates. The fact was that they came into Tibet when travel between Ladakh and Tibet was free, and until the abolition of the Local Government of Tibet by the Chinese in the wake of the disturbances of March-April, 1959, local regulations did not require them to register as Indian nationals or hold official identity certificates. With the Chinese now in complete control of Tibet, they became anxious to register themselves as Indian nationals or alternatively return home. But the Chinese, who claimed them as Chinese nationals, did not permit them to do either. They were even prevented from making contact with the Indian Consul-General at Lhasa for purposes of either consultation or registration. Off and on they were also threatened with dire punishment unless they denounced their claim to Indian nationality and accepted Chinese citizenship. The government of India made repeated representations to Peking on these and other matters, but without much avail.[8]

Side by side with these efforts to tighten the screws on Tibet, the Chinese now began a new series of intrusions across India's traditional northern frontier. On July 30, 1959, the government of India received information regarding the presence of a Chinese armed detachment in Indian territory in the region of Western Pangong Lake in Ladakh and of the establishment of a Chinese camp at Spanggur, both these places lying well within the Indian frontier. News was also received that an Indian police party of six men on reconnaissance duty within the Indian frontier was arrested and taken into custody by the Chinese. The Indian government immediately lodged a strong protest to Peking against the violation of the Indian border and the arrest of the Indian police party "engaged in bonafide duties within Indian territory." Peking, however, instead of answering the Indian protest, brought forward countercharges against India, alleging that Indian armed personnel had intruded into Chinese territory, and as they did not withdraw in spite of "friendly warning," there was no alternative but to disarm and detain them.[9]

This was soon followed by other and more violent intrusion. On August 7 a Chinese patrol, approximately 200 strong, crossed the Indian border at Khinzemare in NEFA. "When encountered by our own patrol who requested the Chinese patrol to withdraw to their territory, our patrol was pushed back to the bridge at Drokung Samba, longitude 91.47′ n."[10] On August 25 another strong Chinese detachment crossed into Indian territory south of Migyitun and fired without notice on an Indian forward picket, killing one person on the spot and seriously wounding another. On the following day the Chinese detachment outflanked the Indian post at Longju, overwhelmed the small Indian force of eighteen men of the Assam Rifles and compelled them to withdraw. When the government of India made a strong protest against this unprovoked firing on a static post within Indian territory, Peking replied: "Longju is indisputably part of Chinese territory," the Indian personnel who were there were guilty of violating Chinese territorial integrity, it was they who had opened fire and the Chinese acted only in self-defense. The Chinese reply added: "no section of Sino-Indian boundary has been formally delimited: . . . the so-called MacMahon Line was set forth in the past by the British imperialists unilaterally and has never been accepted by the

Chinese Government; it of course cannot be regarded as legal."
The note closed with a somber warning: "No violation of
Chinese territory will be tolerated. All areas that have been
invaded and occupied must be evacuated. Any armed provoca-
tion will certainly meet with Chinese frontier guards' firm re-
buff."[11]

If Tibet had, in some measure, shaken Nehru's faith in China,
Longju for the first time made him apprehensive about Chinese intentions toward India. In his desperate longing to main-

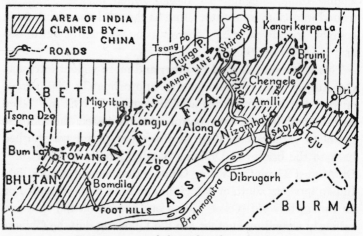

Eastern sector of the India-China frontier.

tain friendship with China, he had for years borne Chinese
intrusions and insults without letting the Parliament or the
country know anything about them. As he himself says in one
of his letters to Chou En-lai: "We did not release to the public
the information which we had about various border intrusions
into our territory by Chinese personnel since 1954, the construction of the road across Indian territory in Ladakh, and the
arrest of our personnel in the Aksai Chin area in 1958 and their
detention. We did not give publicity to this in the hope that
peaceful solutions of the disputes could be found by agreement

between the two countries without public excitement on both sides".[12]

After Longju, it was no longer possible or desirable to keep back the facts about Chinese aggression from the Parliament or people of India. On August 28, 1959, in reply to a series of questions and adjournment motions in the Lok Sabha, Nehru revealed that the Chinese had been continually violating Indian territorial integrity and these intrusions had occurred in places as far apart as Ladakh in the northwest and NEFA in the extreme northeast. He gave a complete account of the Longju incident and announced that the entire NEFA border, which had hitherto been guarded by the Assam Rifles and the militia, would henceforth be placed under army control. He also re-affirmed his earlier policy statement that any aggression against Bhutan and Sikkim would be considered as aggression against India. "While I do not wish to take an alarmist view of the situation," he said, "we should naturally be prepared for any eventuality and without fuss or shouting keep vigilant."[13]

Three days later (August 31), speaking to the Rajya Sabha, Nehru gave a more concrete account of the policy which his government would follow in dealing with Chinese incursions. It would be a "double policy," he said. The government would strengthen border defenses and repulse further incursions and at the same time hold themselves in readiness to "settle matters by conference."[14] In other words, he would not lead the country to war in order to recover the areas which had been forcibly occupied by the Chinese. For this he would employ the methods of negotiation. Any fresh incursion, however, would be repulsed with force.

But there was a logic behind Chinese intrusions, and a part of it was soon revealed. On September 8, 1959, Chou En-lai sent a long note to Nehru, stating that China refused to recognize India's northern frontier and laying claim to about 50,000 square miles of Indian territory. He contended that the Sino-Indian boundary had never been formally delimited; that the central government of China did not send anybody to participate in the conclusion of the treaty of 1842, which delimited the Ladakh-Tibet frontier, and therefore the treaty was not valid; that the section of the boundary consisting of the area of Sang and Tsungha, southwest of Tsaparang Dzong in Tibet, was "30 to 40 years back gradually invaded and occupied by the British" and, therefore, "an outstanding issue left over by history;" and that the "so-called MacMahon Line was a product of British policy of aggression against the Tibet Region of China," and therefore "an illegal line." Chou En-lai added that if China had not yet fully crossed the line and taken possession of territories which she claimed, it was only "to facilitate negotiations." This, the Chinese Prime Minister emphasized, in no way implied that China recognized the traditional frontier.[16]

At long last Chou En-lai came out with what possibly had been in his mind all these years. From 1954 to 1959 he had been pretending that the inflated Chinese maps were mere reproductions of old maps, produced by that "bandit" Chiang Kai-shek, and they were still current because the new regime had had no time to revise them. When Nehru had raised the question of these maps at Peking in 1954 and again at New Delhi in 1956-57, he was solemnly assured that although the Chinese government disliked the use of the phrase "MacMahon Line," they did not entertain any intention to dispute it. But now in September, 1959, Chou En-lai claimed all those Indian territories shown in "bandit" maps as Chinese.

True, this was not the first occasion Chou En-lai gave an inkling of his mind to Nehru. In a letter dated January 23, 1959, he had told the Indian Prime Minister that "there are certain differences between the two sides over the border question," and these related to both Ladakh and NEFA. Lest Nehru might wonder why this question should be raised after so many years of tacit acceptance, Chou En-lai pointedly stated that he had not raised it earlier, "because the conditions were not ripe for settlement."[16] Conditions were indeed not ripe! Motorable roads connecting China with Tibet and then on to the Indian frontier had not yet been built, airfields had not yet been constructed, colonization of Tibet by Chinese immigrants had not yet gone far enough, and, finally, the backbone of the Tibetan nation had not yet been completely broken. In other words, the Chinese deemed it expedient to refrain from raising the question of the frontier until they had consolidated their hold over Tibet and transformed it into an effective base of operations. By September, 1959, such transformation was well under way, and Chou En-lai could now reveal without hesitation some of the ambitions which had been revolving in his mind during the past decade.

Communists and fellow travelers in India were thrilled by the prospect of approaching "liberation." But Nehru was stupefied. In his letter to Chou En-lai, dated September 26, he wrote:

I must frankly say that your letter of the 8th September has come as a great shock to us. India was one of the first countries to extend recognition to the People's Republic of China, and for the last ten years we have consistently sought to maintain and strengthen our friendship with your country. When our two countries signed the 1954 Agreement in regard to the Tibet region, I hoped that the main problems which history had bequeathed to us had been peacefully and finally settled. Five years later, you have now brought forward, with all insistence, a problem which dwarfs in importance all that we had discussed in recent years and, I thought, settled.[17]

In this letter, which in many ways is of historic importance, Nehru maintained that the boundaries of India were settled for centuries "by history, geography, custom and tradition," and he produced a vast array of historical and factual data in support of his statement.[18]

Discussing Chou En-lai's letter in the Parliament, Nehru said that it had created a situation of "serious concern" to India. The Chinese demanded "the Himalayas being handed over as a gift. This was an extra-ordinary claim; and whether India existed or not, this could not be done." He compared the Chinese attitude with that of those aggressive, imperialist powers of the West, who not long ago regarded themselves as leaders of the world and expected the rest to follow them. "What is happening in China today is the pride and arrogance of might that is showing in their language and in their behaviour to us and in so many other things they have done." "What we have to face today," he said in another context, "is a great and powerful nation, which is aggressive. It might be aggressive minus communism or plus communism. Either way it is there." Nehru now realized that his assessment of China, on which India's China policy was based, was wrong. In a depressing tone he confessed to the Parliament that "the Chinese had valued India's friendship only to a very low extent in the final analysis." With disarming frankness, he told his critics: "I did not know that China would behave like this.[19]

Regarding the policy to be pursued in the face of Chinese threats and claims, he told Parliament that while the Mac-Mahon line was India's frontier, he would be prepared for minor adjustments here and there. "A particular place one mile this side or that side of the MacMahon line was a small matter." The broad principle was the watershed. "I stick to that broad approach. But if a slight deviation by evidence or facts in alignment is necessary, it is not a major matter. That has to be decided by facts, not by anybody's coercion.[20] To Chou En-lai he wrote to the same effect, saying that while the government of India could not discuss with China the future of large areas of Indian territory which China claimed, they would be prepared to discuss minor adjustments here and there. "No discussions," however, "can be fruitful unless the posts on the traditional side of the Indian frontier now held by the Chinese forces are first evacuated by them and further threats and intimidations immediately cease."[21]

In the meanwhile, another outburst of anti-Indian vitupera-

tion was let loose in China. Hastily a meeting of the Standing
Committee of the Chinese National People's Congress was
summoned, and every member spoke in support of the claims
put forward by Chou En-lai and expressed "great surprise at
Mr. Nehru defending British imperialism." This support of
"the aggressive plot of British imperialism," said Chou En-lai,
did not "accord with the Five Principles advocated by Nehru."
The Chinese press again raised a hue and cry that the Indian
"reactionaries" were using the Dalai Lama as "a tool against
China."[22]

At Lhasa General Chang Kuo-hua declared that there was
no question of vacating the areas China had occupied.[23]

At the same time the Chinese intensified their activities in
Tibet, along the frontier, and even inside India. With feverish
haste jeepable roads were built to the main passes along the
MacMahon Line, and existing pony and mule tracks were improved. New airstrips on the other side of the line were constructed, and air reconnaissance was intensified all along the
frontier.[24] Within India, against all canons of approved international practice, the Chinese Embassy in New Delhi began to
publish and circulate bulletins criticizing Nehru's statements
and the Indian government's policies, reproducing the texts
of speeches made in the Standing Committee of the National
Peoples' Congress and reprinting anti-Indian articles published in the *People's Daily* of Peking. At the same time, the
Chinese Trade Agency in Kalimpong commenced disseminat-
ing propaganda material, either directly or through the agency
of their Indian sympathizers in the vital border areas of Sikkim
and Bhutan.[25] And, to cap the climax as it were, the Indian
Communist Party intensified its pro-China activity. Pro-Chinese
demonstrations were held in Calcutta and other places, and the
Party's so-called "intellectuals" told the country and their
youthful followers that the Chinese were perfectly right when
they stated that the border between India and China had never
been delineated, that "Socialist China can never commit an act

of aggression," and that "the much publicised intrusion on the Indian border is nothing but a bogey raised by newspapers and a deep-rooted conspiracy by Western imperialists and vested interests."[26]

And then for a brief spell the clouds seemed to lift. The Indian Ambassador at Peking, who hitherto had been deliberately kept at a distance and whose requests to see the Chinese Foreign Minister were repeatedly turned down under one pretext or another, suddenly became an object of extreme friendliness on the part of the Chinese authorities. At Lhasa the guards in front of the Indian Consulate-General were removed and Indian officials were allowed to move about with comparative freedom. On the occasion of the tenth anniversary of the Chinese People's Republic Nehru sent a message of congratulations and good wishes to the Chinese Prime Minister. In reply Chou En-lai sent to the Indian Prime Minister a telegram, couched in the warmest language, applauding the principles of coexistence and describing the current differences between India and China as "only an episode" in a story of "age-old friendship." Mr. Ajoy Ghosh, Secretary of the Indian Communist Party, on his return from Peking and Moscow, testified to the unalloyed friendship of the Chinese for India and their anxiety to work for a peaceful settlement of the border dispute. Some other foreign visitors to Peking came back with the same impressions. Dr. Subandrio, the Indonesian Foreign Minister, stated that "he was sure" the Chinese government wanted to settle border issues with India "peacefully as soon as possible." Dr. Tulsi Giri, Nepal's Development Minister, also made a statement of identical content, adding that his country was willing to offer its good offices to help forward a settlement.[27]

New Delhi was elated. It began almost to expect that China would recant and make some dramatic gesture of good will. Nehru waved aside the suggestion of a defense pact with Pakistan, though negotiations on other matters which began at that time engendered an atmosphere of unprecedented friendliness.

Everything was done to play down the conflict. Nehru declared that he did not believe there was any considered policy behind Chinese action. In the United Nations the leader of the Indian delegation, Mr. Krishna Menon, once more spoke with some vehemence for the admission of Communist China to the China seat in the Security Council and opposed the inclusion of the Tibet question in the General Assembly's agenda, stating, as was stated in 1950, that his government believed that "the plight of the Tibetan people would be resolved by processes of peaceful reconciliation."[28]

But this renewed attempt at reconciliation was cut short by another severe blow. On October 21, 1959, New Delhi got the staggering news that an Indian police party on routine patrol duty near Kongka Pass in the Chang Chemmo valley in Ladakh had been ambushed and fired upon by Chinese troops. The circumstances leading to this tragedy and its aftermath were soon revealed. On October 20, two Indian policemen and a porter went out on patrol duty in the Kongka Pass in Ladakh. When they failed to return in the evening, a party was sent out in search of the missing persons, but the search proved unavailing. On the following morning, therefore, another party under the direction of a senior officer named Karam Singh went out to continue the search. After they had gone about five miles to the east of the Hot Springs they saw the hoofprints of some horses obviously belonging to the Chinese. Following these marks for six or seven hundred yards, they noticed on their left "a Chinese soldier on the hill shouting something and waving his hands upwards as if he was asking us to raise our hands and surrender." Karam Singh shouted back at the top of his voice "that it was our area." Immediately there was a volley of fire both from the front and from the hilltop. The Indian personnel fired back in self-defense, but were overwhelmed by the strategic situation and the superior strength and fire power of the Chinese troops. Whereas the Indian policemen had nothing but rifles with them, the Chinese were provided with rifles, mortars and hand grenades. Nine Indians were killed, one was seriously injured, and others surrendered.

The area where the incident took place is mountainous and uninhabited and about forty to fifty miles west of the traditional Sino-Indian frontier as shown in Indian official maps. It was the practice of Indian frontier guards to proceed to the area once a year to carry out normal patrol duty. But in the months following the patrolling of June, 1958, the Chinese had edged forward from their military base at Rudok and planted their outpost in this neighborhood.

After their surrender the Indian policemen, living, wounded, and dead, were taken by the Chinese to their outpost. One wounded policeman was left on the way and was later unaccounted for. The prisoners were kept in torn tents in bitterly cold weather and without any bedding for five days. In consequence of this, the leader of the party, Karam Singh, and three constables were severely frost-bitten. One of the prisoners who had a bullet wound received no medical attention until the fourth day. Besides, the prisoners were subjected to continuous interrogation from the time of their arrest till the time of their release. They were asked under threats and pressure to make statements to the effect that the Indian party had gone forward knowingly into Chinese territory, that they were the aggressors and that they had sent two constables and a porter on the previous day for purposes of espionage.

In the exchange of notes between the two governments, following the tragedy, Peking complained that "Indian troops" had "unlawfully intruded into Chinese territory" and "opened heavy fire on Chinese frontier guards and launched armed attack." "Under these conditions," the Chinese note of October 22 said, "the Chinese frontier guards were compelled to fire back in self-defence."

In its note of October 23, the government of India repudiated the Chinese allegations, affirmed that the area where the incident occurred was far within the traditional Indian frontier, and maintained that the attack was launched by the Chinese. The note added:

> The Government of India reserve the right to claim adequate compensation from the Chinese Government when the precise extent of the loss is known. The Chinese authorities have no right to arrest or detain Indian personnel who should immediately be released. Further, the Government of India ask the Chinese authorities to withdraw their forces from this area and to prevent their illegal entry into Indian territory and interference with Indian personnel.

The Chinese government in their turn repudiated the statements and demands of the Indian government. Their note of October 25 said:

> . . . the Chinese Government absolutely cannot agree to the allegation of the Indian Government that Chinese troops intruded into Indian Territory and attacked the Indian troops. . . . The Indian side must be held fully responsible for the incident. . . . The place where the Indian troops launched armed provocation is indisputably Chinese territory. . . . Any violation of China's territory is absolutely impermissible and any armed provocation must be firmly rebuffed.

The note also rejected India's claim to any kind of compensation but intimated China's willingness to release the captured Indian policemen and hand over to Indian authorities the dead bodies of those who were killed.

The government of India in its memorandum of November 4 put forward a mass of evidence to prove that the area under dispute really belonged to India. "It is true that the Government of India did not open any border outposts right along the traditional frontier. This was because the area was inhabited very sparsely, if at all, and they had no reason to suspect any aggressive intention on the part of the Chinese Government. They were, therefore, content with sending regular patrol parties to these areas in previous years." In this and a subsequent note the Indian government also placed on record its emphatic protest "against the deplorable treatment to which the Indian personnel were subjected while in the custody of the Chinese soldiers. This treatment which the Indian personnel received was much worse than that to which even prisoners of war are entitled under the Geneva convention of August, 1949."

On November 14, 1959, the birthday of Prime Minister Nehru, the Chinese handed over the dead bodies and released the Indian prisoners.[29]

chapter 8

DELHI SUMMIT

THE KONGKA PASS incident brought India-China relations almost to a breaking point. Indian public opinion was so inflamed that there was a demand from certain quarters that diplomatic relations with Peking be forthwith broken off and that the aggressors be ousted from Indian soil, if necessary by force. Even the Indian policy of non-alignment, which had hithero received the almost unanimous support of the Indian people, now came in for criticism and even men of the stature of Shri C. Rajagopalachari pleaded for an open alignment with the West. For a moment Nehru's own position seemed to be tottering. For the first time since independence, his replacement was openly suggested by some normally loyal and responsible newspapers. "Let us warn him," said a leading English daily of New Delhi, "that he may not have many more opportunities to unite the country behind him, if China is allowed to go on heaping contumely and humiliation on us."

The Indian government, although not in favor of immediate

drastic steps, nevertheless took the gravest view of the situation. The Chinese Ambassador was summoned to the External Affairs Ministry and given a strong note of protest. The Chief of Army Staff and other high-ranking service officers were consulted. An emergency meeting of the Cabinet was held, and decisions were taken to put the Ladakh frontier, like the NEFA frontier a few weeks earlier, under Army control. New border posts were set up, and new measures undertaken to meet any situation which the Chinese might create in future. "Our policy towards China has to be revised to deal with the situation effectively," said President Dr. Rajendra Prasad, presiding over a conference of state governors at New Delhi. Nehru gave an assurance that past mistakes would not be repeated and that India would no longer take chances with her borders in the north and northwest. Should the necessity arise, he added, India would not hesitate to talk in the only language which the Chinese seemed to understand—that of force—for the defense of her territorial integrity.[1]

Meanwhile there was a strong criticism in the world press of Chinese actions in the Indian borderlands. Practically the entire non-Communist press in East, Southeast and West Asia voiced sympathy for India and condemnation of Chinese aggressiveness. And so did the press in western Europe, America, and even Communist Yugoslavia. Even the Kremlin, aware of the harm that Chinese policy was doing to the cause of Communism in Asia, appeared to be perturbed. Mr. Khrushchev gave the British labor leaders, who had met him in the autumn of 1959, the impression that "he was embarrassed and irritated by the Chinese behavior towards India." In a major policy speech to the Supreme Soviet a few days later, the Soviet Premier declared that the Soviet Union would be happy "if there were no more incidents and if the existing frontier disputes were settled by way of friendly negotiations."[2]

Under this pressure of world and in particular of Soviet

opinion, and aware of the growing determination on the part of India to fight rather than surrender, Peking now decided to change its tactics and pursue its objectives in a new form. These tactics consisted primarily in attempting to isolate India diplomatically from some of her Asian neighbors. China had long-standing border disputes with Burma and Nepal and a "nationality" dispute with Indonesia. Negotiations were now set on foot to bring a speedy settlement of these disputes so that Southeast Asian countries (apart from those which were already members of the SEATO) should not forge a united front directed against China. Secondly, attempts were made to "show up" India—to prove to the world that China was in dead earnest about settling her border dispute with India and if it could not be solved, it was entirely due to Indian intransigence.

To drive home this conviction Chou En-lai, without abating his claims by an iota, began now to press for an early meeting between himself and the Indian Prime Minister. In his letter dated November 26, 1959, he formally proposed to Nehru that "the Prime Ministers of the two countries hold talks in the immediate future."[3] It was obvious that no talks could be held so long as the border clashes continued. To ensure border tranquillity during the period of negotiations, he therefore proposed "that the armed forces of India and China each withdraw 20 kilometers at once from the so-called MacMahon Line in the east, and from the line up to which each side exercises actual control in the west, and that the two sides undertake to refrain from again sending their armed personnel to be stationed in and patrol the zones from which they have evacuated their armed forces."[4]

It was not easy for Nehru to accept either the proposal for an immediate meeting or the suggested interim measures for border pacification. There was a strong public opinion in the country that there should be no negotiations with the aggressor so long as he did not "vacate his aggression." Not many weeks ago he himself had given expression to such an opinion. So far as the suggested interim measures were concerned, they were clearly of the nature of a trap. If accepted, they would place China in a position of relative advantage. For, even after withdrawing twenty kilometers from her present position, she would still remain deeply entrenched within Indian territory in the Ladakh region, whereas India would have to fall back further on her own soil in both western and eastern sectors of the border. Moreover, a withdrawal of twenty kilometers all along the frontier would compel India to abandon her old line of check-posts and create a new line in the rear. This would be a tremendously difficult task in view of the nature of the terrain and might involve in practice a fall-back of fifty or sixty miles in some sectors. True, Chou En-lai's proposals, if accepted, would lead to the creation of a demilitarized zone, but it would be done entirely at the expense of India.

Nehru therefore suggested alternative proposals for border pacification and decided to wait on events. In the northeast, he proposed, the MacMahon Line should remain the Indian frontier, and there should not be the slightest risk of any border clash if each government would instruct its outposts not to send out patrols. "It is only when armed patrols go out in these difficult mountainous areas that there is likelihood of clashes taking place." "We have instructed our border outposts," Nehru added, "not to send out any forward patrols for the present. The risk of border clashes will be completely eliminated if our suggestion is accepted by your Government."

As regards Longju, Nehru suggested a compromise. The Chinese should withdraw from Longju, but India would not reoccupy it even though she was quite definite that it was on her side of the MacMahon Line. In the middle sector of the frontier touching Uttar Pradesh, Himachal Pradesh, and Panjab, there were no Indian border areas under Chinese occupation, and there should be "no risk of border clashes if the precaution is taken not to send out border patrols." In regard to the Ladakh sector, Nehru proposed that India would withdraw all her personnel to the west of the line shown as the international boundary in Chinese maps of 1956, and China on her part should similarly withdraw all her personnel to the east of the international boundary as shown in India's official maps and described in Indian notes. "As the two lines were separated by long distances, it was clear that there would hardly be any risk of border clashes between the forces on either side."

In his letter dated December 17, 1959, Chou En-lai rejected Nehru's counterproposals as "lacking in fairness." Their acceptance would mean withdrawal from Aksai Chin, Chang Chenmo Valley, Spangur, Khurnak Fort, and such other areas as the Chinese had either stealthily or forcibly occupied during the last two or three years. Nevertheless Chou En-lai went on repeating his plea for an early meeting between the two Prime Ministers. This disagreement about interim measures, like other disagreements on broad questions of fact, he maintained, was precisely the reason why an early meeting should be held "so as to reach first some agreements of principles as a guidance to concrete discussions and settlement of the boundary question by the two sides." To clinch the issue further, he suggested December 26 as the date on which he and Nehru should meet either in China or in Rangoon.[5]

With no agreement regarding interim measures and complete disagreement concerning fundamental historical facts, Nehru did not see what purpose would be served by a meeting between the two Prime Ministers. "I do not see," he wrote to Chou En-lai on December 21, "how we can reach agreement on principles when there is complete disagreement about the facts." He would not, therefore, proceed to China or Rangoon "within the next few days." Yet he thought it prudent to keep the doors open for negotiations. In the same letter, he told Chou En-lai: "I am always ready to meet and discuss with your Excellency the outstanding differences be-

tween our countries and explore the avenues of settlement.
. . . I would however prefer to wait for your promised reply to
my letter of September 26 and our note of November 4 before
we discuss what should be the next step."[6]

The promised reply of the Chinese government was published by the Chinese Embassy at New Delhi on January 3,
1960. Although the longest note ever sent from Peking to New
Delhi, it contained little beyond a reiteration of the earlier
Chinese arguments and Chinese version of the historical data
in support of Chinese claims to 50,000 square miles of Indian
territory. There was not the slightest indication that the Chinese government intended to vacate the areas in NEFA and
Ladakh which they had forcibly occupied, for in their view
these areas, besides many more, belonged of right to them.
But there was nevertheless a repetition of the plea for an early
meeting between the Prime Ministers. "In view of the fact that
the Sino-Indian boundary question is rather complex and that
it would be extremely difficult to bring about a settlement
through the exchange of letters, the Chinese Government has
always maintained that face-to-face talks should be held
speedily between the representatives of the Governments, first
of all between the Prime Ministers of the two countries, so as
more effectively to exchange views and reach agreement."[7]

It was now crystal clear that there was no basis for negotiations. A brochure released by the Ministry of External Affairs
on January 13, 1960, unequivocally declared that the government of India "cannot accept the Chinese contention that the
entire India-China frontier was undelimited. Negotiations on
this basis are unacceptable to the Government of India."
About the same date Nehru told a press conference at New
Delhi that there was no common ground between the Chinese
and Indian points of view, and therefore he did not visualize
any meeting between himself and the Chinese Prime Minister
in the near future.

Hardly three weeks had passed when India was startled by

the news that Nehru had invited Chou En-lai to a meeting at New Delhi. What led to this unexpected shift in policy is not known. It is possible that Nehru was a little unnerved by the propaganda capital which was being made in certain quarters of his refusal to meet Chou En-lai unless certain conditions were satisfied. Initiated in some East European capitals, this propaganda was steadily filtering into Southeast Asian countries. It is more probable that Soviet influence had something to do with this *volte-face*. On January 20 there had come to New Delhi on a two-weeks' visit some distinguished visitors from the U.S.S.R.—President Kliment E. Voroshilov, First Deputy Chairman of the U.S.S.R. Council of Ministers, Mr. F. R. Kozlov, and a Deputy of the U.S.S.R. Supreme Soviet, Madame Ye. A. Furtseva, and doubtless they had pro-longed discussions with the Indian Prime Minister about the current deadlock in India-China relations.[8] Understandably Nehru wanted to be on the right side of the Soviet Union, while he was so much on the wrong side of China. But his invitation to Chou En-lai was taken with ill grace by large sec-tions of the Indian press and some sections of the Indian Par-liament. Minoo Masani described it as a "national humilia-tion." "It does not add to the dignity of our country," said Acharya Kripalani, "that our Prime Minister should change his position so soon and so suddenly without an explanation or even an excuse." Nehru defended himself by saying that he had invited Chou En-lai "for a meeting and not for negotia-tions"!

Chou En-lai needed no persuasion to accept the invitation. In a sense it was for him a diplomatic victory. A meeting with-out preconditions was what he was pleading for. He had got it. Intimating his acceptance of the invitation on February 26, 1960, he wrote, "The Chinese Government . . . takes a positive attitude towards the forthcoming meeting and has confidence in it. . . . I particularly hope to see the dark clouds hovering between our two countries dispersed through our joint efforts so that the long-standing friendly relations between our two countries may be consolidated and developed."[9]

On April 19 Chou En-lai arrived at New Delhi, accompanied by Marshal Chen Yi, Vice-Premier and Minister for Foreign Affairs; Mr. Chang Han-fu, Vice Foreign Minister, and Mr. Chang Yen, Deputy Director of Foreign Affairs under the State Council. In a frank and firm speech of welcome at the Palam airport, Nehru stated how the relation between India and China had been "imperilled in the present and for the future and the very basis on which they stood has been shaken." In his reply Chou En-lai referred to the age-old friendship between India and China. "Our two peoples have been friendly to each other over thousands of years in the past. We shall remain friendly to each other for the thousands and tens of thousands of years to come." That being so, he added, "there was no reason why this question between us cannot be settled reasonably through friendly consultations in accordance with the Five Principles."

But platitudes and shibboleths did not help in resolving the deadlock. For six days Chou En-lai and his colleagues conferred with Nehru and other high functionaries of the government of India, but the clouds did not disperse. Basic disagreement about historical and actual facts came up again and again during the discussions. There was no movement from fixed positions, no acceptable formula for the liquidation of the dispute. A joint communiqué issued on April 25 admitted that "the talks did not result in resolving differences that had arisen." As a face-saving device, however, the two Prime Ministers agreed that "officials of the two governments should meet and examine, check and study all historical documents, records, maps and other material relevant to the boundary question . . . and draw up a report for submission to the two Governments." Two days later (April 27), Nehru stated in the Lok Sabha that the official teams had no authority or competence to deal with the problem except that they could examine and list facts presented by each side. He added that he did not anticipate any significant advance in finding a solution to the dispute from the coming talks between the two official teams.

On the eve of his departure from New Delhi, Chou En-lai held a press conference in which he gave some indication of a bargain which he wanted to strike with Nehru but did not succeed. There was already a hint of this in Peking's note of December 26, 1959, in which special emphasis was laid on the importance, from the Chinese point of view, of the Aksai Chin highway as a vital line of communication between Tibet and Sinkiang. In the press conference Chou En-lai said, "as China was prepared to accommodate the Indian point of view in the eastern sector, India should accommodate China in the western sector." Again: ". . . the so-called MacMahon Line is absolutely unacceptable to China. Nevertheless we are willing to maintain the present state of that sector of the boundary. We will not cross that line. . . . We hope that the Indian Government will take [toward the western sector] an attitude similar to that which the Chinese Government has taken towards the eastern sector, an attitude of mutual accommodation."

This seems to have been the essence of the "positive attitude" with which Chou En-lai had come to India. But the bargain was not acceptable to the Indian government. Speaking informally to newsmen at the Palam airport, where he had gone to see Chou En-lai off on the morning of April 26, Nehru declared that there could be no question of "barter" in such matters. The same day in the Lok Sabha the Prime Minister stated that prolonged discussion with Chou En-lai had come up against "the rock of entirely different sets of facts." While the Chinese claimed that they had been in "constructive" and "actual" occupation of the area in Ladakh, India maintained that the area belonged to her and the Chinese came into it in the last few years. A New Delhi commentator probably hit the mark when he wrote: "The Chinese came to blackmail us into accepting the illegal gains they have achieved by aggression as the price of withholding for the time being their claims to another 40,000 square miles of our territory. Withholding, not renouncing. . . . There was no question of the Chinese abandonment of their claim to the rest of Ladakh. All that was available to India was a provisional agreement offering a freeze on China's other territorial claims in return for the conferment of legitimacy on the territory under Chinese occupation."[10]

Whatever the reasons, this Asian summit fared no better than its European counterpart, and for very much the same reason. In both cases there was no adequate diplomatic or lower-level preparation. Yet the Delhi meeting was not a complete failure. It led to a temporary lessening of tensions, there being an understanding that the *status quo* would not be disturbed at least so long as the examination of documents by the two official teams continued. Moreover, as Nehru stated in the Indian Parliament, the meeting enabled the Indian leaders to gain "a clearer perception of the Chinese mind." It gave India a breathing-spell to prepare for the worst, if and when it came. On the other hand, it gave the Chinese time to consolidate their holdings and make preparations for the next step.

In the months following the Delhi meeting, the two official teams met first at Peking in June-July, then at New Delhi in August-September, and finally at Rangoon in November-December, 1960. As anticipated, nothing fruitful emerged out of this prolonged examination of documents and maps. Reporting to the parliament on December 21, Prime Minister Nehru stated that the joint report of the Chinese and Indian official teams really consisted of "two reports" with hardly anything in common between them.

Meanwhile neither India nor China was sitting idle. Despite financial difficulties India undertook an elaborate program of road construction in vital Himalayan areas. Defensive measures of other kinds were also undertaken along the frontier. China too was busy constructing new motorable roads and airfields, creating new military outposts along the frontier, and, according to some unconfirmed reports, setting up rocket bases on the Tibetan plateau. There was mounting evidence of intense reconnaissance activity, of trespasses into Indian territory by Chinese personnel, of violations of Indian air space by Chinese aircraft, and of growing infiltration in the Indian border regions. Speaking to the Rajya Sabha on August 19, 1960, Prime Minister Nehru told the House that China had for months been carrying on a violent anti-Indian propaganda, that reports of Chinese military build-up in Tibet were true, and that the Indian Communists were engaged in an "unpatriotic" and "most anti-national" campaign in the border regions.

chapter 9

CHINESE CLAIMS EXAMINED

THE BORDER dispute between India and China thus bids fair to become one of the most intractable problems of contemporary Asian politics. In the long-drawn wordy debate which has accompanied the dispute, the one thesis on which the Chinese have harped almost *ad nauseam* is that the Sino-Indian frontier had never been delimited. It is not clear, however, what the Chinese meant by delimitation. If they meant delineation on a map, they are obviously wrong; for a large number of maps published in various countries, including China, showed the alignment of the Indo-Tibetan boundary as in official Indian maps, thus proving that the traditional frontier had been well known and recognized. If, on the other hand, they meant demarcation on the ground, they are largely right. For the Indo-Tibetan border in all its length, except for the small part between Sikkim and Tibet and a portion of the Garhwal frontier, was never demarcated on the ground. This has been so mainly because in most parts the frontiers traverse high, almost inaccessible mountainous terrain, the main

124

axis of the High Himalayan Range, and they were easily recognizable from description of unchanging natural features, reinforced by custom and tradition.

The Indian thesis, on the other, has been that even if not demarcated on the ground, the traditional Indo-Tibetan frontiers had been well known for centuries, and with one or two exceptions had never been challenged by any previous government of Tibet or China. These frontiers, according to the Indian view, being based on the geographical principle of watershed, run along the natural dividing line between India and Tibet; they have the sanction of centuries of tradition and custom; and they have in large parts been reinforced by treaties and agreements between the governments of Kashmir and India on the one hand and those of Tibet and China on the other. In support of this thesis the Indian government has put forward a huge mass of evidence, customary, traditional, historical, geographical, administrative, and cartographic, which the inquisitive reader may read with profit in the pages of the *White Papers* and the *Report of the Officials of the Governments of India and the People's Republic of China on the Boundary Question*. They have not only produced extracts from ancient chronicles and historical works, travelers' accounts and memoirs, texts of treaties and agreements, maps from various countries, official and unofficial, showing the correct boundary along the traditional line; they have also supplied systematic and detailed documentary evidence of revenue settlements, census operations, land taxes, official tours, and other aspects of general administration which go to show that the Indian authorities had at least for many decades, if not for centuries, exercised effective administrative and civil jurisdiction up to that line.

As compared to the wealth of evidence produced by the Indian side, the evidence brought forward by the Chinese is not only "scanty in character" but often "internally inconsistent both in facts and arguments." It is significant that in the course of discussions with Indian officials, the Chinese were unable to provide accurate information regarding the points through which their line ran, showing that they were not even familiar with the topography of the territory which they claim to have possessed and administered for centuries. Equally significant is the fact that even in Chinese official maps published since the inauguration of the Communist regime the delineation of the boundary with India has not been consistent. The 1951 and 1959 maps, for instance, show the delineation in one way, while the 1954 and 1956 maps show it in a wholly different way. In presenting what little documentary evidence they could in support of their stand, the Chinese relied heavily on British sources, often failing to understand their true significance and sometimes deliberately attempting to misinterpret passages from books and documents without reference to their context; but when the government of India presented more significant and unchallengeable British documents in support of their case, the Chinese dismissed them as "imperialist" and unworthy of notice. The Chinese even described some official Chinese maps (such as that of Hung Ta-chen of 1893 and the Postal Maps of 1917, 1919, and 1933) which show the boundary along the Indian alignment, as "imperialist."

In fact, being conscious of the weakness of their case, the Chinese have shown more concern in trying to demolish the Indian thesis than in substantiating their own. Their arguments are often of a negative character because they have no adequate positive evidence to justify their extravagant claims.

Let us now proceed a little more into details. For convenience of discussion the Indo-Tibetan frontier may be divided into three sectors: (A) the northwestern sector consisting of the boundary between Ladakh and Tibet; (B) the central sector covering the boundary between Panjab, Himachal Pradesh, and Uttar Pradesh, on the one hand, and Tibet on the other; and (C) the northeastern sector extending from the northeastern tip of Bhutan to the Isu Razi pass on the northwest of Burma.

(A) In the first or northwestern sector the Chinese have laid claims to about 33,000 square kilometers of Indian territory, and as stated already, have seized about 12,000 square kilometers. The main arguments they have put forward in support of their claims are as follows:

(i) The treaty of 1842 between Maharaja Gulab Singh of Jammu and Kashmir on the one hand and the Dalai Lama and the Emperor of China on the other, on which India partially bases her claims to the present international frontier, is not valid in law because neither did the Chinese Central Government send anybody to participate in the conclusion of the treaty nor did they ratify it.

(ii) The frontiers between Ladakh and Tibet were never delimited, as is shown by the fact that "down to 1899 the British Government still formally proposed to delimit this section of the boundary with the Chinese Government but the latter did not agree."

(iii) Some early British maps show the alignment of the frontier more or less as in recent Chinese maps. "Later British and Indian maps included large tracts of Chinese territory into Ladakh."

(iv) The 1842 treaty "was concluded between the authorities of the Tibet region of China and the Kashmir authorities; but the greatest part of the area (about 80 per cent) now disputed by the Indian Government is part of China's Sinkiang which was no party to the treaty."

(v) Chinese sovereignty over a large part of the disputed area has been proved by the construction of the Tibet-Sinkiang highway even without the knowledge of the government of India and the apprehension, arrest, and shooting down of Indian trespassers in 1958 and 1959.

(vi) The names of some of the areas which the Chinese claim, such as Aksai Chin and Karakash, are of Uighur origin. This is an additional proof that the areas belong to China.

None of these arguments will bear scrutiny.

(i) This point is a complete distortion of historical facts.

We have elsewhere given some of the essential details of the 1842 treaty. It is clear from the text of the treaty, cited in that context (Chapter 5) that the "Khagan of China" was as much a party to it as the Lama Guru Sahib of Lhasa. Moreover, the treaty bears the signature of one Kalon Sokon, who, although a Tibetan by birth, nevertheless held a Chinese rank. Peking's contention that the Chinese Central Government was no party to this treaty and sent no one to participate in its conclusion is thus untrue. Whether the treaty was ratified or not is not clear. It is possible that this custom of modern international law had not yet come to be regarded as an essential condition of valid treaty-making in those remote, secluded, mountainous regions of the world in the early decades of the nineteenth century. But even if not formally ratified, it is clear from the note written by the Chinese Amban at Lhasa to the British government on January 13, 1847, that the Chinese government recognized the treaty and fully accepted its provisions.[1] In fact, for well over a century, the validity of the treaty was never questioned by any Chinese government until the Communists came into power in China and reconquered Tibet. It is part of the Communist game to detach Ladakh from Jammu and Kashmir and make it again a part of the "Tibet region of China."

(ii) This argument is equally incorrect. There is no record of any proposals having been made by the British government between 1847 and 1899. In the latter year, the British did make a proposal, but it was with reference to the northern frontier of Ladakh with Sinkiang and not the eastern frontier of Ladakh with Tibet. In connection with this proposal it was clearly stated that "the northern boundary of Ladakh ran along the Kuen Lun range to a point east of 80° east longitude, where it met the eastern boundary of Ladakh." This proves beyond doubt that Aksai Chin was a part of Indian territory.

(iii) Regarding maps, the general position is just the reverse of what the Chinese seem to imply. It is true that in a map of

"Punjab, Western Himalaya and adjoining parts of Tibet" compiled by Walker and published in 1854, the boundary of Ladakh is shown more or less as in contemporary Chinese maps. But this map was drawn up at a time the British government in India knew little about the eastern or northern parts of Ladakh. It may be noted that they had assumed sovereignty over the Jammu and Kashmir state, to which Ladakh belonged, only a few years earlier and their knowledge of the more inaccessible regions of Ladakh was inevitably imperfect. But before long they began to send a series of exploration and survey parties into eastern and northern Ladakh, in consequence of which it became possible to ascertain the exact lie of the watershed along which the traditional frontier lay. More accurate maps then began to appear; and from 1865 onward all British Indian maps show the frontiers of Ladakh as they are today. Official Chinese maps of the late nineteenth century also showed the frontiers more or less along the same lines. It is only as the twentieth century progressed that the Chinese gradually changed their maps so as to include large parts of Ladakh. But even then all Chinese maps did not show the frontier in the same way. For instance, in most Chinese maps Chang Chenmo Valley is shown outside the boundary of the Tibet region of China. But Peking has nevertheless forcibly occupied it.

(iv), (v), (vi). These points, which were raised as a kind of afterthought, may be more speedily dismissed. The statement in (iv) that 80 per cent of the disputed area in Ladakh was part of Sinkiang in 1842 is contradicted even by Chinese maps of the eighteenth and nineteenth centuries, which show that Sinkiang never extended south of the Kuen Lun mountains. With reference to (v), it may be stated that stealthy or forcible occupation does not automatically invest the occupant with the rights of ownership. Number (vi) is the queerest of all the Chinese arguments. In putting it forward the Communists obviously forgot that there are many place names in Tibet and Sinkiang which are of Sanskrit or Prakrit origin. The name Khotan, for instance, is derived from the Sanskrit word Kustana. Will China give up its claim to this ancient land because it bears a name derived from Sanskrit? Or will China surrender Manasarwar and Kailas to India because these holy places in Tibet, revered by Hindus from all over India, bear typically Indian or Sanskritic names?

(B) In the central sector, the Chinese claims involve a comparatively much smaller area, but include localities which occupy a special place in Indian traditions and sentiments. Here in the upper valleys between two roughly parallel ranges of snow peaks are located some of the most sacred sanctuaries visited by streams of Hindu pilgrims for countless generations.

The areas which the Chinese claim are the Spiti region, Nilang-Jadhang, Bara Hoti, Sangcha Malla, and Lapthal. With regard to the Spiti area, the Chinese contend that it had always been part of China, but was "occupied or intruded into by India only after the signing of the 1954 Sino-Indian Agreement." As against this the government of India has pointed out that the traditional frontier in this area is "the major watershed between the Pare Chu and the Spiti systems," and the Spiti area is on the Indian side of the watershed. Moreover, until a few years ago the Chinese recognized this area as belonging to India. Even a wall map of the People's Republic of China published in November, 1953, showed this territory within India.

Nilang-Jadhang is very close to the source of the Ganges at Gangotri. A copper-plate inscription of 1667 shows that this territory, which originally belonged to the Bushahr state (now in Himachal Pradesh), was transferred to the Tehri state under the terms of a treaty concluded in that year. Since that date it had continued to be a part of the Tehri state, but in 1949 when the Tehri state was merged in the Uttar Pradesh it came under the administration of the Uttar Pradesh government. It is thus clear that Nilang-Jadhang has at least for some centuries been a part of India.

Bara Hoti (called Wu-je by the Chinese) is a very small area (about 1½ square miles), situated between the main watershed of the Sutlej and Alakananda, which is the boundary in this sector. It has been shown as a part of India in Indian maps since 1860, "when maps of this region based on surveys were first drawn." In its controversy with India over this area, China initially contended that it was 12 kilometers north of the Tunjun La (a border pass), while India maintained that it was two miles south of the pass. And it was then agreed that if Bara Hoti was to the north of the pass, India would surrender its claims over it; but if it was to the south it would be treated as Indian territory. When China later discovered that it was really to the south of Tunjun La, she went back on the agreement and contended that, no matter where its location might be, "it is within Chinese territory."[2]

The two other contested areas, Sangcha Malla and Lapthal, are situated in the Almora district in Uttar Pradesh on the Indian side of the Balcha Dhura pass, which is the traditional boundary between India and Tibet in this area. No Chinese map has ever shown these places within Tibet, whereas all Indian maps and documents have shown them as Indian since at least the third quarter of the last century.

Aside from the above, there is also a controversy between India and China regarding the ownership of the six boundary passes mentioned in Article IV of the Sino-Indian Treaty of 1954. These six passes are Shipki La, Mana, Niti, Kungri, Bingri, Darma, and Lipu Lekh, all situated in this region. India claims ownership of the southern ends of these passes on the ground that they lie to the south of the watershed, the natural and traditional frontier, and they are mentioned in the agreement without any reference to Chinese ownership. China rebuts a part of the Indian argument by stating that the 1954 agreement does not deal with the question of boundary at all, which is true. Then to prove its own ownership it puts in a plea which is at once dangerous and fantastic. The plea is that the people living in the debatable areas are mostly of Tibetan origin. All along the Himalaya peoples of Indian and Mongoloid stocks have lived for centuries side by side, and in most areas they are inextricably mixed. Apart from the difficulty of drawing an ethnic frontier in this tangled mosaic of races, it should be borne in mind that ethnic considerations have never been the only ones in frontier-making. If the Chinese can claim these areas on the ground that their people are mostly of Tibetan stock, by an extension of the same reasoning they may also claim Ladakh, Bhutan, Sikkim, and parts of Nepal. This is possibly what the Chinese have in mind. Statements made by Chinese officials in Tibet, refered to above, confirm the same impression. But, in the ultimate analysis, every demand for an ethnic frontier is based on the principle of self-determination of peoples. China, which conquered Tibet by methods of violence and terror in 1950 and again suppressed with fire and sword the national upsurge of the Tibetans in 1959, can hardly invoke this noble doctrine in support of its claim for an ethnic frontier. That would sound like the Devil muttering the scriptures.

(C) Northeastern sector. In this sector the Chinese claim some 90,000 square kilometers of Indian territory including the whole of NEFA and parts of Assam. They have based their claim on the following grounds:

(i) The MacMahon Line was an "illegal line"—a product of the British policy of aggression against the Tibet region of China. It was "illegal" because (a) it was not discussed at the Simla conference but was determined by British and Tibetan representatives "behind the back of the representative of the Chinese Central Government" and (b) the Simla convention of 1914 was not ratified by the Chinese Central Government.

(ii) Prior to 1937 even British Indian maps did not show the Indian frontier along the MacMahon Line but rather along the alignment shown in Chinese maps.

(iii) Until recently the area down to the plains of Assam was under Chinese jurisdiction.

We may consider these points one by one.

(i) In a previous chapter we have already stated the main facts about the Simla conference and one of its products—the MacMahon Line. It was a tripartite conference held specifically to decide the question of Tibet and settle its frontiers. On August 7, 1913, the Foreign Minister of China wrote to the British representative that the Chinese plenipotentiary would proceed to India "to open negotiations for a treaty jointly with the Tibetan and British representatives." The plenipotentiaries of the three governments—Mr. Ivan Chen from China, Mr. Lonchen Shatra from Tibet, and Sir Henry MacMahon on behalf of British India—met on a footing of perfect equality and exchanged copies of their credentials on October 13, 1913. The credentials of the Tibetan representative were issued by the government of the Dalai Lama and not by the Chinese government. They made it clear that Tibet was an equal party at the conference with the right "to decide all matters that may be beneficial to Tibet," and the Chinese plenipotentiary accepted the credentials as being in order.

The full proceedings of the Simla conference have not yet been published. It is probable, however, that so far as the Indo-Tibetan frontier was concerned, it was in the first instance negotiated between the Tibetan and British representatives for the simple reason that in 1914 China could hardly have had a say in the matter. But when the draft convention emerging from the conference was presented on April 22, 1914, for signature by the three plenipotentiaries, it had attached to it a map showing the boundary line between Tibet and India as well as the lines between Inner Tibet and China and Inner Tibet and Outer Tibet. The Tibetan border towards India and China was marked by a red line and that between Outer and Inner Tibet by a blue line. And then to eliminate any possibility of doubt, Article VI of the convention stated: "For the purpose of the present Convention the borders of Tibet and the boundary between Outer and Inner Tibet shall be shown in red and

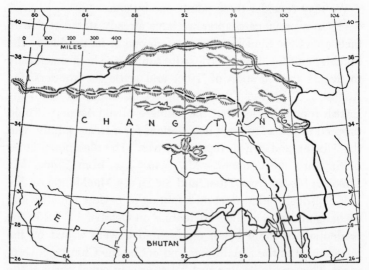

Map initialed by the plenipotentiaries at the Simla Convention, with a solid line indicating the Tibetan border toward India and China and a broken line marking the border between Outer and Inner Tibet.

blue respectively on the map attached thereto." The Convention was initialed by the three plenipotentiaries and the map initialed by the British representative and signed by the Tibetan and Chinese representatives as a token of their acceptance.

In view of the above facts, to say now, as the Chinese have been saying, that the "Tibet local authorities had no right to enter into talks or conclude treaties on its own with foreign countries,"[3] or that the MacMahon Line was an "illegal line" because it was determined by the British and Tibetan representatives "behind the back of the Chinese Central Government" would appear to be preposterous. Even more preposterous is the plea put forward by Chou En-lai in his letter to Nehru dated December 26, 1959, that the red line on the map toward India "was presented as the *boundary between Tibet and the rest of China,* and it was never stated that part of the red line was the boundary between China and India."[4] This would imply that the Assam foothills to the south of the Himalayan axis belonged not even to Tibet but to China and the red line in the south was introduced to mark off Himalayan Indian territories of China from Tibet proper![5]

It is true, as stated earlier, that the Simla convention was not ratified by China. But when announcing its refusal to ratify the convention, the Chinese government stated that its only objection to the treaty was the issue of the frontier between Outer and Inner Tibet. It never raised any question about the proposed Indo-Tibetan frontier. On June 13, 1914, the Chinese government submitted a memorandum making fresh proposals regarding the frontier between Inner and Outer Tibet. Even in that memorandum there was no Chinese objection or criticism of the MacMahon Line boundary. Almost five years later, on May 30, 1919, the Chinese government again "suggested some modifications with a view to reaching some final settlement." These suggested modifications also did not include any reference to the Indo-Tibetan frontier.

The fact is that in 1914 and for decades thereafter China was not in the least interested in the Indo-Tibetan frontier. Tibet was then free. She had thrown off the last vestiges of Chinese suzerainty. Her relations with China were marked by acute bitterness and hostility. It was thus only natural for China not to worry about any supposed loss of territory by Tibet to the then government of India. The conclusion thus seems irresistible that the arguments now put forward by Red China are in the nature of an afterthought designed to bolster up new expansionist ambitions.

(ii), (iii). The two remaining arguments put forward by the Chinese in support of their territorial claims in the northeast sector do not appear to be any more cogent than the one we have considered. The position regarding maps relating to the

northeast frontier is thus explained by Sir Olaf Caroe, Foreign
Secretary to the Government of India from 1939 to 1945:

In the early days of British rule the external frontiers of India
were conceived as lying at the limits of the territory where British
writ ran. But on the North-east, as on the belt known as the North-
West frontier, there lay beyond the limits of administered territory
an agglomeration of tribes owning no master. In such cases it became the practice of the early British administrators to exercise
in the region beyond the administered border what was known
as a loose "political" control. "Trans-border" agencies were set up,
but it was not until later that the need was felt to show the tribes
so politically controlled as excluded from the neighbouring states
and included in India.

Thus there was a time-lag in amending the maps. On the
North-West Frontier they were amended after the Durand Line
was delimited in 1893. On the North-East frontier, the Mac-
Mahon Line having been accepted by Tibet—without a Chinese
demurrer—there was a greater time-lag in amending the maps,
mainly because the First World War supervened and MacMahon
himself was sent to Egypt in 1914. But the new position will be
found clearly set out in Volume XIV of Atchison's Treaties, 1929
edition. The maps were amended thereafter.[6]

The other Chinese contention, that until recently the area
now comprised in NEFA down to the plains of Assam was
under Chinese jurisdiction, is contradicted by known historical
facts. From about the middle of the last century, some of the
tribes living in NEFA area began to enter into agreements
with the government of India, accepting some kind of loose
political control by the latter over them. Thus agreements were
signed with the Akas in 1844 and 1888, with the Abors in
1862-63 and 1866, and with the Monbas in 1844 and 1853. In
the early years of the present century, as already mentioned,
surveys were carried out in the area up to the southern limits
of Tibetan jurisdiction, and the Sadiya and Balipara Frontier
Tracts covering the area now known as the North-East Frontier

Agency were formed in 1912 and 1913. It will thus be seen that the Chinese contention, referred to above, is without foundation, and that the MacMahon Line merely put a coping-stone on a historical process which had been in operation for at least three quarters of a century. In the words of Prime Minister Nehru, it only "formalised the natural, traditional, ethnic and administrative boundary in the area."[7]

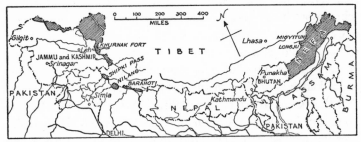

Latest Chinese map superimposed over an official Indian map, showing the 50,000 square miles of Indian territory (shaded) claimed by the Chinese. The Indian border is indicated by the broken line, and the one claimed by the Chinese is shown by the solid line.

But behind all these arguments used by the Chinese in support of their claims is another of a more fundamental character. They have reconquered Tibet; and all that belonged to Tibet at one time or another must of right belong to them. The modern Indo-Tibetan (Sino-Indian in current parlance) frontier was primarily set up by the British. "Using India as its base, Britain conducted extensive territorial expansion into China's Tibet region, and even the Sinkiang region." This is what Chou En-lai wrote to Nehru in his letter dated September 8, 1959.[8] "The eastern and western sectors of the boundary line," ran another Chinese note of December 26, 1959,

are the product of the British policy of aggression and expansion in modern history. . . . While embarking on armed aggression against Tibet and conspiring to cause Tibet to break away from

China, Britain also nibbled at the frontiers of Tibet both on the maps and in deed, which resulted in the boundary line that was later inherited by India and is marked on current Indian maps.[9]

Britain has now withdrawn from India, whereas China has re-appeared in Tibet in the fullness of her power. It is, therefore, fitting that what was done by Britain must now be undone. Old landmarks set up or confirmed by the British must be replaced by new landmarks designed by China. And in the new scheme of things India, which detests Western imperialism, must consent to the Chinese design in the interest of Asian solidarity and as a mark of Asian resurgence. Did not Nehru consent to the liquidation of the rights and privileges which India had inherited from the British in Tibet on the ground that they were "relics of imperialism"? Why then cling to "the boundary line which Britain unlawfully created through aggression against Tibet"?[10] True, there were some treaties between British India and Tibet or British India, Tibet, and China. But "many dirty unequal treaties signed by the past Chinese Governments have already been proclaimed null and void." There is, therefore, no reason why old Sino-Indian or Indo-Tibetan treaties should not go the same way.[11] This is the burden of the Chinese song—the basic argument, albeit half concealed, behind the entire barrage of other arguments put forward by Peking to bolster up its claims to 50,000 square miles of Indian territory.[*]

[*]Materials for this chapter have been mostly taken from the *White Papers* and the *Report of the Officials of the Governments of India and the People's Republic of China on the Boundary Question.*

chapter 10

RETROSPECT AND PROSPECT

WITH NO settlement in sight, India and China seem
to be poised on the brink of a conflict that might lead to un-
foreseen and unpredictable consequences. This rapid deteri-
oration in Sino-Indian relations, in sharp contrast to the
previous romantic phase, has been a puzzle to most publicists
and political commentators. Why did China, it has been
asked, abandon her former policy of apparent friendship with
India and adopt one of open hostility? What is the real logic
behind her intrusions and claims? What is the rationale behind Peking's aggressive posture?

Of the many answers that have been given to this question,
by far the most naive and uninformed is that which attributes
this shift in Chinese policy to the widespread expression of
Indian sympathy for the distressed Tibetans and the political
asylum given by the government of India to the Dalai Lama
and his followers in 1959. One need only turn the pages of the
White Papers published by the Indian government to see
that a whole series of Chinese actions antedated the Tibetan

revolt. These included Chinese intrusions into Indian territory, the construction of the Tibet-Sinkiang highway through Aksai Chin, and the circulation of Chinese maps showing large chunks of Indian territory as Chinese. The first letter of Premier Chou En-lai to Prime Minister Nehru stating that "the Sino-Indian boundary had never been formally delimited," and that the MacMahon Line was "a product of the British policy of aggression against the Tibet Region of China" and could not therefore "be considered legal," preceded the revolt in Lhasa by at least seven weeks. Only the world did not know anything about this growing friction, for Prime Minister Nehru kept it concealed "in the hope that peaceful solutions to the disputes could be found by agreement by the two countries without public excitement by both sides."

Another widely held view is that the adoption of an aggressive policy toward India was prompted by the need to divert the attention of the Chinese people from the failures of the Communists on the home front. Peking had previously asserted that it had constructed a series of dams and carried through other projects, which would make impossible any recurrence of droughts and floods in China. The hopes thus roused were belied by later events. In 1959 there occurred a series of national disasters which brought the country almost to the brink of famine. Party leaders were then compelled to admit that their previous claims were a little too optimistic, that the figures given were often exaggerated, and that the majority of the projects were carried out with such haste that they could not possibly withstand the onslaughts of nature. Coming as they did in the wake of the economic dislocations caused by the spurt in 1958, particularly in transportation, the failure of the widely-advertised backyard blast furnaces, and the strains and problems created by the nation-wide communization of villages, these admissions inevitably led to acute disappointment in the country, and Mao thought it expedient to divert the attention of the people by pursuing a policy of adventure abroad. Such a policy, the Communist leaders possibly believed, would have the effect of subverting India's Five-Year Plans and arresting her economic progress. It would compel India to increase her defense budgets at the cost of her development projects.

It has also been contended by some observers that Peking's aggressive posture was motivated by its anxiety to sabotage Premier Khrushchev's efforts to reach a *détente* with the West, particularly the United States of America. The Chinese Communists, it has been argued, resented the Kremlin's efforts at settlement with the West without their own participation and without their interests being taken into full consideration, and were therefore anxious to create a situation which would serve as sand in the gears of understanding and settlement.

But perhaps the most plansible explanation of Chinese behavior is that Peking is pursuing the traditional Chinese policy of expansionism. Every strong imperial regime in China has in the past attempted to expand its borders. There has been a revival of this historic trait now that China is again strong, its government centralized and its life and thought completely regimented.

One may expand this explanation a little more fully. China's long history and imperial tradition have bred in its people a deep sense of cultural superiority and a belief in China's natural primacy in Asia.[1] The very name China in Chinese is the Middle Country—for millennia the only highly cultured and civilized entity in the whole of East Asia—surrounded by miscellaneous barbarians who oscillated in alternating subjection and hostility round the Great Within. Communist China has inherited this sense of primacy as a legacy from the past. And understandably she seeks to revive the old glory and recreate her old primacy. The Communists believe that China's traditional superiority, reinforced by her recent

accession of strength, entitle her to play the role of a para-
mount power in Asia and a major power in world affairs.
Chou En-lai insisted that Peking's views must be heard in the
settlement of any international issue, and the Chinese press
claimed that no settlement of any international problem,
any Asian problem in particular, is possible without the participation of the Chinese People's Republic.[2] To recreate
China's primacy in Asia, the first essential was to extend
Peking's hegemony over all those regions and peoples which
once belonged to the Chinese empire or remotely recognized
its overlordship. Hence the conquest of Tibet, the fortification
of Chinese rule over Sinkiang and Inner Mongolia, and
Peking's quest for dominance in Korea, Indochina, Burma,
Malaya, Nepal, and Bhutan. The second essential was to
erase from memory all humiliations and defeats of the past.
Hence the eagerness to repudiate all treaties which are
reminiscent of China's past weakness. The third essential
was to give the people a new sense of pride and might.
Hence the deliberate attempt to liquidate Buddhism and
Confucianism, the former because it breeds pacifism and the
latter because it teaches self-doubt and humility.

But China's ambitions are not limited to the revival of
former Chinese supremacy; she is seized with a revolutionary
zeal to reshape the map of the world in the Communist pattern. Steadily accumulating evidence suggests that ideological convictions have a stronger hold on the Chinese mind
than on the Russian; and it seems possible that the center of
Communist orthodoxy may in the foreseeable future shift
from Moscow to Peking. As custodians of the "true faith," the
Chinese believe in the "inevitability" of the world revolution
and the ultimate triumph of Communism all over the world.
And like orthodox Communists elsewhere they consider it to
be their primary duty to hasten the process of that revolution.
In pursuit of this objective all tactics are legitimate and all
double talk justified. Wars waged in pursuit of revolutionary

aims are sacred. "Some people have ridiculed us as the advocates of 'omnipotence' of war," wrote Mao in his *Problems of War and Strategy*. "Yes, we are; we are the advocates of the omnipotence of the revolutionary war, which is not bad at all, but is good and is Marxist."[3]

More than once in recent years Mao has also given expression to his conviction that war between the East and the West is inevitable, that a decisive shift in the world balance of power has taken place in favor of the Communist bloc, and that the latter must enhance its inner consolidation and strike while the iron is hot. "I consider that the present world situation has reached a new turning point," Mao said on November 18, 1957, before a gathering of Communist parties at Moscow. "There are two winds in the world, the east wind and the west wind. There is a saying in China: 'If the east wind does not prevail over the west wind, then the west wind will prevail over the east wind'. I think the characteristic of the current situation is that the east wind prevails over the west wind; that is, the strength of socialism exceeds the strength of imperialism."[4] This assessment of the balance of power in the world, along with ideological frenzy, may be at the root of much of Chinese truculence and militancy in world affairs. Even nuclear war does not seem to have that terror for the Chinese mind that it has, for instance, for the Russian. "Modern revisionists," said General Li Chih-min in June, 1960, "have exaggerated the consequences of the destructiveness of nuclear war." The Chinese have even challenged Khrushchev's thesis that there will be no victors in the case of a nuclear war. "The results will certainly not be the annihilation of mankind. Over the debris of the dead imperialism, the victorious people would create very swiftly a civilisation thousands of times higher than the capitalist system and a truly beautiful future for themselves."[5] There should, therefore, be no inhibition against war even in this nuclear age, provided it is waged for revolutionary purposes. If in the process Peking's hegemony is extended, it will only add to the glory of the revolution. Sultan Mahmud of Ghazni destroyed and plundered the temples of Hindustan to exalt the glory of Islam; the added glory of Allah was manifested in the untold riches which he accumulated in the process.

These, then, are two of the most dominant factors in the contemporary Chinese scene. Militant nationalism and the revolutionary zeal of Communism lie deeply embedded in the foundations of Mao's China. And as Max Beloff points out in another context, this marriage between an ethnic or territorial power-complex and an ideology (divine or secular) has always in the past created a formidable combination.

Aside from the above, a few other factors must be taken into consideration in forming an assessment of Communist China. China not only occupies nearly one-fourth of the giant Asiatic land mass, but, like Germany in Europe, she also occupies a central position within the Asian continent. This makes it possible for her to expand in all directions, nibble at the frontiers of weaker neighbors, and terrorize them by means of pressure. It is well known that China and Chinese minorities are a burning problem to most of the countries on its periphery—from Korea and Japan to Formosa, Indonesia, Laos, Malaya, and Burma. Secondly, China has a population of 650 million increasing at the rate of 2.4 per cent annually. Experts on population problems have computed that if present trends continue the Chinese population will be 700 million in 1963, 800 million in 1968, and a billion by 1980. This huge and rapidly growing population "has been organised, regimented and mobilised in support of the revolutionary goals set by Peking's new leaders."[6]

Thirdly, China has an army which is not only the largest in Asia but the second largest in the world. The strength of this army is usually estimated at two and one-half million men, with another half a million security troops in the background. In large measure, this army is stocked with Soviet equipment and supplies. Besides this huge army, China has millions of partially trained militiamen throughout the country and tremendous reserves of military manpower. Of even more sinister significance than the size and strength of the army is the fact that the nation has in a fundamental sense been militarized. The Chinese Communist Party, as a secret Soviet document recently pointed out, "has grown up as an army and not as a civilian organisation like any other communist party."[7] Naturally under its leadership, "military virtues and military men have been elevated to a position of new prestige in Chinese society, and the population of the country has been fully mobilized to support the military establishments."[8]

Finally, the rapid economic growth of China in the past decade has steadily strengthened Peking's base for military power and improved its relative position in world affairs. Although some of their claims regarding production increases have been found to be wrong, and the pace of development is obviously generating new stresses and strains, there is a general agreement among competent observers that economic growth in Communist China is proceeding at an exceedingly rapid pace. In fact Communist China's rate of economic growth appears to be much faster than that of India, and in a few years Peking will have built a base of heavy industries almost overshadowing that of Japan.

China thus has or is tending to have all the ingredients which make a nation a menace to others—an advantageous geographical position, an inherent superiority complex, a rapidly increasing population which needs *lebensraum,* a powerful army with a rapidly expanding industrial base, and, finally, a militant ideology which gives the Chinese a supreme confidence in their ultimate victory. In tactics, China has the advantages of a highly centralized dictatorship, assisted by vast fifth columns abroad and an extensive and effective propaganda system within and ouside the country. It has also the disadvantages which stem from a rigid bureaucracy, from the dissatisfaction of an overstrained, semi-enslaved people (as was evident in the short spell of the "hundred flowers"), and from the necessity, at least in part, of relating tactical changes to basic ideological aims and motives.

With all these factors, however, Peking might not have become an immediate danger to India but for Tibet. Chinese occupation of Tibet carried with it the seeds of future conflict with India. Even before the Communists came into power in mainland China, they viewed India with deep suspicion on account of her friendly sympathy toward Tibet and her special relations with Sikkim and Bhutan. They looked upon Nehru as a "stooge" and "hireling" of Western imperialism and as one who "shamelessly holds himself as the pillar of the anti-Communist movement."

The India of Nehru [wrote a commentator in *World Culture* of Shanghai, September 16, 1949] attained dominion status only two years ago, and is not even formally independent in the fullest sense of the word. But Nehru, riding behind the imperialists whose stooge he is, actually *considers himself the leader of the Asian peoples*. Into his slavish and bourgeois reactionary character has now been instilled the beastly ambition for aggression, and he thinks that his role as a hireling of imperialism makes him an imperialist himself. *He has announced that Bhutan is an Indian protectorate,* and now proceeds to declare that "Tibet has never acknowledged China's suzerainty" in order to carry out his *plot* to create incidents in Tibet.

"Under the long standing influence of British imperialism, the bourgeois of India, of whom Nehru is the representative, have learned the ways of imperialists *and are harbouring intentions against Tibet and Sikkim as well as Bhutan.* Furthermore Nehru, to curry favour with his masters, the Anglo-American imperialists, is placing himself at their disposal, and shamelessly holds himself as the pillar of the anti-Communist movement in Asia.

The writer then proceeds: "As a rebel against the movement for national independence, as a blackguard, who undermines the progress of the people's liberation movement, and as a loyal slave of imperialism Nehru has already been made the substitute of Chiang Kai-shek by the imperialists."

Other press comments contain vitriolic attacks on Nehru on account of his initiative in holding a non-official Pan-Asian conference in March, 1947, and another Asian conference in January, 1949.

In his assumption of the role of the vanguard in the international gamble against the peoples of Asia, Nehru has committed a series of malicious intrigues, all following the victorious march of the liberation movement of the Chinese people. As early as the days prior to India's "independence," Nehru had called a Pan-Asian Conference. . . . Early in 1949, Nehru called another Asian Conference in New Delhi, outwardly with the motive of mediating in the Indonesian dispute, but actually for undertaking a preliminary discussion of South-east Asian alliance. On February 28, 1949 Nehru, nominally to mediate in the Burmese civil war, called a conference of the British dominions, the real purpose of which was to discuss the strengthening of measures for the Anti-Communist alliance in South-East Asia . . . and so on up to the recent act of Nehru in serving as the hireling of Anglo-American imperialism in the attempt to invade Tibet. . . .[9]

Extracts like these from the Chinese press of 1949 and 1950 may be multiplied: but those cited are enough to indicate the working of the Chinese mind in relation to India a decade ago. It is clear that the deep suspicion and bitterness of the Chinese Communists toward India were primarily due to (i) India's deliberate preference to continue as a democratic country and her failure to join the Communist bloc, (ii) her relations with Sikkim and Bhutan, (iii) her friendly sympathy toward Tibet and its people, and (iv) her attempt at leadership in Asian affairs from time to time.

This last point needs a little elaboration. We have noticed in an earlier chapter how the Chinese attitude toward India underwent a fundamental change soon after India became independent. A free India was welcome; but a free India making a bid for Asian leadership was a different proposition. In this matter the Chinese red, white, or pink are all alike. But more than the Kuomintang, the Chinese Communists saw in India their strongest potential Asian rival. Here was a country with as proud a past as China's, though without the Chinese expansionist traditions. It had all the potentialities of becoming a great power in future. Were it a Communist country, it might have been possible to come to terms with it in the interest of international Communism. But it had adopted Western democratic institutions; its leaders believed in Western liberalism; its government followed a policy of non-alignment in international affairs. What was even more intolerable in Chinese eyes was that smaller nations in South and Southeast Asia looked to India as an example, and for advice, guidance, and help. Peking could not afford to tolerate a rival for the Asian mind—an Asian obstacle in the way of her grand designs. Comments in the Chinese press since 1959 prove that this basic attitude of the Chinese Communists has not fundamentally changed, in spite of all that has happened in the meantime.

The Chinese conquered Tibet in 1950. But Tibet was only the first step in China's *drang nach süden*. Even before the "liberation" of Tibet, as the press comments quoted above show, the Communists looked askance at India's relations with Sikkim and Bhutan. Soon after "liberation," they gave a clear indication of their intention to follow it up by the "liberation" of Ladakh, Nepal, Sikkim, and Bhutan. These were described as "the four teeth with which the Chinese will grind their way to the Southern Seas."

In the following years Chinese policy followed a zigzag course. For a short span, Peking changed its tactics in the belief that a smiling face would serve its purpose better than a frowning face. It would disarm suspicions; it would secure much-needed help in the wider field of international affairs; above all, it would keep the enemy napping while the

Chinese built the base. Hence the frequent exchange of good-will and cultural missions, the constant reiteration of the "age-old" and "eternal" Sino-Indian friendship, the *Panch Shila* agreement and the Bandung accord. But Peking never lost sight of its long-term aims.

"When our two countries signed the 1954 Agreement in regard to the Tibet region," wrote Nehru to Chou En-lai on September 26, 1959, "I hoped that the main problems which history had bequeathed to us in the relations between India and China had been peacefully and finally settled. Five years later, you have now brought forward, with all insistence, a problem which dwarfs in importance all that we have discussed in recent years and, I thought, settled."[10] The Indian Prime Minister obviously forgot that Peking's leaders did not believe in freezing a situation or permanently solving a problem with non-Communist countries. They signed the agreement of 1954 because they deemed it necessary to stabilize the situation temporarily so that they might prepare better for the next leap forward. Chinese intrusions and claims since 1954, following a well designed pattern, represent that leap forward.

What are the Chinese driving at? Possibly a base in the southern slopes of the Himalayas so as to be able, when the time is ripe, to "grind their way to the southern seas." Extension of Chinese rule in the sub-Himalayan belt would clearly place them in a position from which they could, when necessary, provide the wherewithal of an armed struggle to the Indian Communists. One of the most important reasons why the Communists succeeded in Indochina, while they failed in other southeast Asian countries such as Malaya or Indonesia, was that China had a common border with the former but none with the latter. This common frontier made it possible for the Chinese to provide the Viet Minh Communists with lavish military supplies and thus ensure their military success. Once the Chinese Communists entrench themselves in a part of the sub-Himalayan belt, the present obstacle imposed by the High Himalayan Range in the way of easy communication with the Indian Communists will be overcome, thus bringing the prospect of Indian "liberation" within the range of practical politics.

The main weakness of India's China policy for almost a decade was that it was based more on what it called wishful thinking than on objective conditions. It is well to remember that Prime Minister Nehru, although primarily a man of action, is also a man of dreams. His dreams are India's asset; they are also its weakness. He considered Sino-Indian friendship a *sine qua non* for Asian and world peace. Speaking to the Lok Sabha in September, 1959, he said: "I have always thought that it is important and essential that India and China have friendly and, as far as possible, cooperative relations. It would be a tragedy not only for India and China but to Asia and the world if these two countries developed some kind of permanent hostility." There could be no two opinions about this unexceptionable proposition. But his eagerness to maintain and promote that friendship made him partially blind to the full implications of Chinese policies and actions.

For years Nehru worked on the hypothesis that Chinese Communism could be contained by tolerance, patience, and friendship. And he made an all-out effort to calm Chinese truculence and to make of China a normal, well-behaved neighbor by offering it his friendly assistance in abundance. The Chinese exploited his friendship but did not give up their truculence. The *White Papers* bear eloquent testimony to Nehru's patience in the face of growing Chinese intrusions since 1954. Every time an intrusion took place, the government of India protested, but withheld events from public knowledge. The Chinese took Nehru's patience for supineness and treated his protests with bellicose contempt. In practically all the communications which Chou En-lai addressed to Nehru on border violations, there is a cynical reference to *Panch Shila* and "age-old friendship," but the emphasis is unmistakably on China's pretended right based on might.

The fundamental defect of India's China policy stemmed from a failure to take sufficient cognizance of Peking's long-term goals. Indeed, when others spoke of the long-run aims of Chinese Communism, India tended to dismiss it as a propaganda stunt, meant to disrupt Sino-Indian friendship and Asian solidarity. This explains India's prolonged negligence in building up an adequate defense system along the northern frontier and developing a network of communications up to the shoulders of the Himalayas. This also explains her critical attitude toward the defenses set up by others against Chinese expansionism. She looked upon those defenses as irritants to Chinese sensibility and threats to Chinese security, and believed that if only they were dismantled or withdrawn, China would settle down to a peaceful career of internal reconstruction.

Historical analogies are often misleading. But India's China policy lends itself to a comparison with the policy pursued by Western statesmen toward Adolf Hitler in pre-Munich years. In both cases, the initial weakness emerged from a misjudgment of long-term intentions. Hitler had given expression to his far-reaching designs in *Mein Kampf*. But as the book was written while he was still an obscure and discredited conspirator, few Western statesmen attached to it the importance which it deserved. *Mein Kampf*, they thought, was the idle outburst of a fanatic, of little significance in relation to the Hitler with whom they had to deal. The consequence was that they tended to attribute Hitler's excesses to the injustices of Versailles and failed to correlate them to the grand designs he had mapped out in his earlier years. And Hitler confounded them by his tactics. After each step forward he declared that it was his last, and that he was now prepared to rest from his labors, at peace with all men. It was only after the rape of Czechoslovakia that the full implications of Hitler's policies were understood by Western statesmen. It was only after the tragedies of Longju and Chang Chenmo Valley and the undisguised revelation of other Chinese ambitions that the implications of Peking's policies were slowly realized by Indian leadership.

There is little doubt that a series of shocks coming in close succession to one another awakened Prime Minister Nehru to the gravity of the peril from the north. Time and again he has referred to the far-reaching implications of the Chinese menace. "The Chinese border attacks," he said in the course of a speech at a mammoth public meeting in New Delhi on November 1, 1959, "constitute a big problem, which could take bigger dimensions in future. I cannot say what form it will take in future, but the dimensions of the challenge may grow. We have, therefore, to meet the challenge not only in its present aspect but also be ready to meet it tomorrow or the day after." Speaking in the Lok Sabha on November 27, 1959, Nehru emphasized that the issue between India and China was of the "biggest magnitude—a matter of the utmost significance to the present and future of India and Asia." "We are sitting on the edge of history," he added, "and all kinds of things are going to happen in the future".

Meanwhile, the nature of the problem posed by China from the other side of India's Himalayan frontier has progressively become more and more manifest. In Sinkiang the Chinese have been building up basic industrial complexes and pushing through a program of transportation development, partly with a view to linking it up with Tibet. Apart from the Sinkiang-Tibet highway (730 miles) through Aksai Chin, which has been a subject of debate between India and China since 1958, China, it is said, has constructed six new roads in the occupied parts of Ladakh. They are also contemplating the linking of Sinkiang with Tibet by rail; when this plan matures, the defense of India will be immeasurably more difficult. In Tibet, three trends can be easily detected in the news filtering through the bamboo curtain. In the first place, a big program of transportation development is being carried through with relentless vigor. Among the truck highways which have been completed the most important are: Sikong-Tibet (1,400 miles), Chinghai-Tibet (1,310 miles), Heiho-Gartok (700 miles), Lhasa-Yatung (390 miles) and Gartok-Pulantsung (158 miles). Other roads have been built along the MacMahon Line and the Nepalese frontier. It is important to remember that these roads are primarily meant for military purposes, and cannot be justified wholly on economic grounds. A chain of about twenty airfields has also been constructed. The largest, at Gartok, is entirely military in nature. A large air force depot at Digacha able to accommodate several hundred planes is only a few minutes by plane from Nepal. Among other airfields one is at Drechen in the Phari Dzong and another at Kala plain in the Unta Valley. Secondly, the Chinese army in Tibet has been increased to 350,000 men, including a chemical warfare unit and three engineering units.[11] This makes a ratio of one Chinese soldier to three Tibetan civilians. Thirdly, Peking has been pouring into Tibet millions of Chinese colonizers in a systematic and ruthless program of absorption and annihilation of the Tibetan people. There are reasons to think that if the present trends continue, within a period of years the Chinese will come to outnumber the Tibetans in Tibet proper and dominate their lives beyond any hope of preserving the Tibetan tradition.

Hand in hand with these developments, pressure on Indian border lands has been growing. But it is more a pressure of sabotage and infiltration than the threat of a full-scale invasion. As indicated before, the Chinese Communists seem to have set their heart on taking over Nepal, Bhutan, and Sikkim, apart from Ladakh and NEFA, at some future date. The logic behind the "liberation" of Tibet is also the logic behind this quest for dominance over these frontier states. Like Tibet, Nepal was at one time tributary to China, and Sikkim and Bhutan were tributary to Tibet. In his dispatch to the Secretary of the government of Bengal, dated April 8, 1861, Ashley Eden, the British Envoy and Special Commissioner to Sikkim, wrote: "Nepal is tributary to China, Tibet is tributary to China, and Sikkim and Bhutan are tributary to Tibet."[12] Like Tibet, Nepal had broken off her last links with China after the fall of the Manchus in 1911. Bhutan and Sikkim were detached from Tibet by what the Chinese would call the British policy of aggression. Now that China is strong, the old wrongs must be righted. Only the *modus operandi* will have to be different in view of the difference in objective conditions. A frontal attack might provoke a major war. Hence the need to pursue sapping and mining operations so as to soften these border lands before the army marches in. With the help of the Indian Communists local grievances must be exploited to the fullest extent to foment anti-Indian sentiments. Local authorities must be brought into contempt through persistent propaganda. Above all, pro-Chinese factions must be created in vital border areas. In other words, all possible techniques must be employed to create conditions in which the Chinese army may cross the border in the guise of a "liberating," not an invading, force.

Nepalese politics since 1950 have been somewhat complex. But among the many factors which have contributed to this complexity, the arrival of China on Nepal's northern frontier may be reckoned as one of the most significant. For one thing, it has subjected Nepal to two pulls instead of one— the old traditional pull from the south, based on geographical historical and cultural ties between India and Nepal, and the new pull from the north, motivated by revivalist, expansionist ambitions. These two rival pulls, coupled with the disappearance of the old reactionary but strong Rana regime in 1950, have introduced an element of uncertainty in Nepalese politics. Whereas India has been mainly concerned in helping Nepal to become a stable state and hence an effective barrier against Communist infiltration, Peking's primary interest has been to eliminate Indian influence and build up Chinese influence in its place. Nepal has in consequence become the cockpit of an unspoken cold war between her two mighty neighbors.

During the first few years after the occupation of Tibet, China was relatively quiescent. For one thing, her hands were full up with the Korean imbroglio; for another, she needed time to consolidate her position in Tibet, her newly acquired forward base. But from 1955 she began gradually to dig her toes into Nepal. The first step was the agreement signed on August 1, 1955, providing for the establishment of diplomatic relations between Nepal and China on the basis of the Five Principles of Peaceful Coexistence. The second step was the Sino-Nepalese Treaty on Tibet signed on September 20, 1956, which *inter alia* provided for the establishment of a Chinese consulate-general in Katmandu and three agencies at suitable points in the interior, in return for similar advantages which Nepal had been enjoying in Tibet since 1856. This was supplemented by an agreement on economic assistance, under the terms of which China offered to pay Nepal a sum of sixty million rupees by way of aid. It is interesting to note that the aid was offered without Nepal's asking for it and at a time when she did not possess the organization even to absorb the aid she was receiving from India.

Almost simultaneously there began an exchange of cultural missions. Peking invited Nepalese officials for formal visits. It brought Nepalese peasants and women to "democratic" and "peace" conferences in China. Nepalese Communists traveled to and fro across the frontier loaded with Chinese propaganda material. Nepal's foreign policy began now and then to exhibit pro-China overtones. In January, 1957,

Premier Chou En-lai paid a visit to Katmandu and told a gathering of Nepalese citizens that "Nepal and China are blood brothers and nothing can poison this relationship."

The government of India has repeatedly stated that Nepal's geographical position dictated a special Nepalese-Indian relationship. This position was recognized in the international community to the extent that the few countries which were interested in Nepal arranged for their diplomatic representatives in New Delhi to be concurrently accredited to Katmandu. The only exception was Great Britain, and that for historical reasons. But in the middle of 1959, when India was preoccupied with the Chinese incursions, the Soviet Union moved with dramatic speed to establish a Soviet embassy in Nepal. This was followed by the establishment of a United States embassy in Katmandu. It was now the turn of Communist China to move in and strengthen the position of the Communist bloc in this vulnerable frontier state. Following a visit by Prime Minister B. P. Koirala of Nepal to Peking in March, 1960, a series of Sino-Nepalese agreements were announced—one providing for the establishment of a joint committee to demarcate the boundary between Nepal and Tibet, another permitting the Chinese to open an embassy at Katmandu, and a third embodying a decision to conclude a treaty of peace and friendship betweeen the two countries. There was also an economic aid agreement. As a measure of good will, China offered Nepal a free grant of 100 million rupees as aid, although 40 million rupees of the Chinese aid of 1956 had not yet been used by the Nepalese government. Under this agreement, Chinese technicians and experts were to go to Nepal to develop Nepalese projects and Nepalese trainees were to go to China for technical training.

Chou En-lai came on a second visit to Nepal in April, 1960, following the failure of the Delhi summit. Replying to a civic reception accorded him in Katmandu on April 26, he declared: "Friendly cooperation between Nepal and China cannot be undermined by any force on earth." On April 28 he told members of the Nepalese Parliament that the Chinese Government "warmly welcome and fully support Nepal's policy of neutrality." On the same day a peace and friendship treaty between Nepal and China was signed.

Meanwhile, anti-Indian feelings in Nepal have steadily grown. The special correspondent of the *Statesman,* after a visit to Nepal, wrote in its issue of March 11, 1961: "China and Russia have very effective lobbies in Kathmandu and elsewhere in Nepal to whip up anti-Indian feeling. There are organisations which are helped with money and ideas. The aim is to dislodge India from the position she holds in Nepal and bring the latter in their sphere of influence." Gone are the days when Nepal could be depended upon to stand by the government of India through thick and thin.

In Sikkim and Bhutan, Chinese pressure has been exerted through more subterranean channels and has possibly made less impression, partly because Sikkim is an Indian protectorate and Bhutan's foreign policy is under Indian control, and partly also because the overwhelming majority of the Sikkimese and Bhutanese are lamaist Buddhists and the fate of the Dalai Lama, the head of the lamaist church, has been to them at once a shock and a warning. But Chinese intentions regarding these states are no longer in doubt. The reader will remember the midnight press conference which the Chinese Premier addressed on the eve of his departure from Delhi in April, 1960. Asked about Sikkim and Bhutan, Chou En-lai said: "We respect India's relations with Sikkim and Bhutan." The transcript of this conference issued in Peking, however, showed this to read: "We respect India's proper relations with Sikkim and Bhutan," the emphasis being on the adjective "proper". In January, 1961, the Maharaja of Bhutan and his Prime Minister disclosed that Peking unofficially approached the Bhutanese government with a request to open direct border talks (in violation of the Indo-Bhutanese agreement of 1949) and an offer of economic aid for the development of Bhutan. It has also been reported that during the official level talks at Peking, Delhi, and Rangoon, the Chinese officials persistently refused to discuss with their Indian counterparts the borders of Sikkim and Bhutan (as also the frontier to the west of the Karakoram Pass). All these are significant pointers to Chinese designs regarding these Himalayan states.

But perhaps more sinister in its implications is the reported move for talks between China and Pakistan for the demarcation of the border to the west of the Karakoram Range. Chinese maps show a part of what is called Azad Kashmir including the Gilgit Agency and a portion of Hunza within the territorial limits of the Chinese People's Republic. But Azad Kashmir, as is well known, is juridically a part of the state of Jammu and Kashmir and, therefore, of the Republic of India. This move, therefore, not only amounts to a recognition by China of Pakistan's sovereignty over Azad Kashmir, but may well be a part of Peking's calculated design to isolate India from her neighbors, Burma, Nepal, and Pakistan. In 1934 Hitler concluded a non-aggression pact with Poland, which marked the beginning of a diplomatic revolution in inter-war Europe. In January, 1960, Communist China concluded a Treaty of Friendship and Non-Aggression with Burma. In April, 1960, she signed a Peace and Friendship Treaty with Nepal. A similar treaty with Pakistan will complete the cycle. Well did Prime Minister Nehru describe (on April 29, 1960) the present tension between India and China as "a drama of which only the beginnings have been seen and no man knows what the end of it will be."

Before we conclude, it may be emphasized that the border problem is not the only problem betweeen India and China. Viewed rightly, it would appear to be no more than a facet of a broader, deeper, long-term contest between Communist China and India—a contest which will determine whether democracy and freedom will survive in Asia or Communism and tyranny will hold sway over this ancient continent. On the political plane the central problem is that of the balance of power in Asia. The emergence of a totalitarian colossus in the heart of the Asian continent has upset that balance. In fact, the challenge posed by Communist China to the free nations of Asia in the second half of the twentieth century is in essence similar to the challenge posed by united Germany to the nations of Europe in the first half. And as years roll by, the challenge is likely to grow rather than abate. In 1823 Canning had "called a new world into existence to redress the balance of the old." The balance in Asia today is maintained by non-Asian forces operating on the Asian scene. It is not, therefore, in the interest of India nor of other free Asian nations to call upon those forces to leave Asia to itself, thus creating a power vacuum which Communist China alone can fill. Nothing will please Peking better than an Asian Monroe Doctrine.

This certainly does not mean that India should give up her policy of non-alignment and enter into some kind of military alliance with the United States of America. In the opinion of this writer an alignment with the West at this juncture may be a serious mistake. It may forthwith bring the Soviet Union behind China; and we shall be confronted with the combined pressure of two giants rather than of one. Until now the Soviet Union has maintained an attitude of neutrality in the Sino-Indian controversy, and this neutrality may not be entirely faked. For it is plainly not in Russian national interest to see China forge ahead with her schemes of expansion and thus become too strong for other powers. Immediately, Chinese expansion will create a widespread revulsion of feeling in non-Communist Asian nations; in the long run, it will create a tremendous problem for the Soviet Union. For if China has ancient claims, pretended or genuine, to a wider hegemony in South and Southeast Asia, she has similar claims to extensive territories under Soviet control. The present Soviet Union comprises about half a million square miles of territory which once belonged to the Chinese empire and has been conquered by Russia since 1840. The recent ideological tension between Moscow and Peking may well conceal in its bosom the seeds of a future Sino-Russian conflict. It may well be the beginning of an inner competition between these two powers for the leadership of the Communist bloc. General de Gaulle of France was possibly not wholly wrong when he stated some time ago that the Soviet Union's problems in Asia were one of the reasons for her seeking an accommodation with the West. A growing rift between the Soviet Union and China is the hope of the future, for India and the world. It is, therefore, not in the Indian interest to retard the development of any such rift by her own precipitate action.

This is not to say that India should build on the hypothesis that such a rift exists or is inevitable in future. For while one set of long-term interests tends to drive a wedge between the Soviet Union and China, another set of short-term interests tends to hold them together. It may be noted that since 1955, despite Indian protests, the Soviet Union has been publishing maps showing the Sino-Indian boundary broadly along the Chinese alignment. Their maps of 1959 have even shown Sikkim and Bhutan as independent states beyond India's northern frontier. While too much stress need not be laid on these "cartographic errors," it may be wrong to ignore them either as wholly without significance. Well did Winston Churchill describe Soviet policy as a riddle, wrapped in mystery and enclosed within an enigma. In the context of current Sino-Indian conflict nothing calls for greater vigilance than the attitudes and policies of the Soviet Union in Asia.

Until there is more positive evidence pointing to Soviet complicity in the Chinese policy of aggression against India, the validity of the Indian policy of non-alignment will remain unassailable. But while adhering to that policy, India can and should promote a closer understanding with the West and, in particular, with the non-Communist countries of East and Southeast Asia. The main task of Indian statesmanship, today and in the immediate future, is to adopt positive measures to fight against Chinese pressure and infiltration across the Himalayan frontier and to promote, indirectly and adroitly, a common policy of defense against Communist China without an open alliance with the West.*

* EDITOR'S NOTE: On November 20, 1961 the Indian government made public a note sent to Peking on October 31 listing eleven Chinese violations of the Indian frontier since April 1960—six in Ladakh, three in Sikkim, and three in the North-East Frontier Agency. India rejected a Chinese note of August 12 charging the Indians with border violations, and asserted that recent Chinese actions "establish conclusively that the Chinese are guilty of further aggression against India." Parliament was much aroused, and opposition members, in particular, demanded stronger action. On November 28 Nehru, asserting that "we do not want war," told Parliament that India was building up her military position to the point where she could take "effective action to recover the lost territories." On the same day the Indian government issued *White Paper* No. V, containing notes exchanged between India and China in the past year. *New York Times,* November 21, 29, 1961.

NOTES

Chapter 1   Historic Friendships

1. *Pacific Affairs*, XIII (1940), p. 19.
2. *Ibid.*, p. 20.
3. *Amrita Bazar Patrika*, April 13, 1936.
4. The letters exchanged between Noguchi and Tagore were published in the *Modern Review* (Calcutta), October, 1938, pp. 486-88.
5. *The Nation*, New York (1942), p. 411.
6. *The Nation*, New York (1942), pp. 411-12.
7. S. Radhakrishnan, *India and China* (Bombay, 1947).
8. *Far Eastern Survey*, XVI (1947), pp. 97-99.
9. Li Tieh-tseng, *The Historical Status of Tibet* (1956), p. 195.
10. *Far Eastern Survey*, XVI (1947), pp. 97-99.
11. K. M. Panikkar, who was Indian Ambassador to both Kuomintang and Communist China, describes the Kuomintang Chinese attitude toward India as follows: "It did not take me long to discover that the Kuomintang attitude towards India, while generally friendly, was inclined to be a little patronising. It was the attitude of an elder brother who was considerably older and well established in the world, prepared to give his advice to a younger brother struggling to make his way. Independence of India was welcome, but of course it was understood that China as the recognised Great Power in the East after the war expected India to know her place. The Foreign Office or the Wai Chiaopu

was the best organised department of the Government and it was here that the doctrine was most firmly held." He adds, however, that "even in regard to America the Chinese attitude was one of patronising condescension." *In Two Chinas*, pp. 26-27.

Chapter 2   Tibet and Its Historical Status

1. *The Communist* (Bombay), January, 1950.

2. K. M. Panikkar writes (*In Two Chinas*, p. 68) that Burma requested India to allow her to be the first and India agreed.

3. Broadcast from Peking radio in English on May 21, 1950.

4. L. A. Waddell, *Lhasa and Its Mysteries*, p. 26.

5. W. W. Rockhill, *Dalai Lamas of Lhasa and Their Relations with the Manchu Emperors of China (1644-1908)*, p. 18.

6. See L. Petech, *China and Tibet in the Early Eighteenth Century*, Chapters III-IV.

7. Charles Bell, *Tibet Past and Present*, pp. 61-62.

8. Sir Francis Younghusband, *India and Tibet*, pp. 421-22.

9. *The Question of Tibet and the Rule of Law*, International Commission of Jurists, p. 79.

10. Charles Bell, *Tibet Past and Present*, pp. 154-55. In regard to foreign relations it was stipulated (Art. 7b) that Outer Tibet would have the freedom of direct negotiation with Great Britain.

11. *The Question of Tibet and the Rule of Law*, p. 86.

12. Erich Teichman, *Travels in Eastern Tibet*, pp. 46-47.

13. Hugh Richardson, *Red Star Over Tibet*, p. 8.

14. *Foreign Relations of the United States*, 1942, p. 145. It should be noted that the U.S. State Department did not fully concur with the British view.

15. 151 *British and Foreign State Papers*, pp. 89-90.

Chapter 3   Communist China Conquers Tibet

1. Thotab, a Tibetan monk from Kham, in the course of a statement to the International Commission of Jurists, recapitulated an incident connected with the Red Army's march to Yenan. "I was 17 years old then," he said. "Chu Teh came to our country via Gyal Rong. They were having a big congregation of monks in the monastery of Tao Ngyam-tso Gompo. The monastery alone houses 1900 monks. The fleeing communists under Chu Teh attacked the monastery, killing 30 monks. The monastery was destroyed and they ran off taking the wealth and animals. On the march they robbed us of our grains and other possessions. Because of this raid the country got famine stricken and thousands died for want of food." *The Question of Tibet and the Rule of Law*, p. 207.

2. Edgar Snow, *Red Star over China* (revised edition), p. 193.

3. See Panikkar, *In Two Chinas*, p. 176.

4. *Ibid.*, p. 105.

5. China had already, in September, 1949, accused India of being party to an Anglo-American plot to oppose legitimate Chinese action in Tibet. *New China News Agency*, September 3, 1949.

6. For full text of notes exchanged between the governments of India and the People's Republic of China, October-November 1950, see *Documents on International Affairs* 1949-1950 (Royal Institute of International Affairs, London), pp. 550-56.

7. For the full text of Tibet's appeal to the United Nations see *Keesing's Contemporary Archives*, 1950, pp. 11102-103.

8. United Nations, General Assembly, Fifth Session, Official Records (General Committee, 73rd Meeting), pp. 17-20.

9. *The Statesman* (Calcutta), December 8, 1950, 5:5.

Chapter 4 India Faces China in Tibet

1. Parliament of India, *Parliamentary Debates, Official Report,* November 20, 1950.

2. In 1951 there were 18 major posts and 15 outposts. By 1954 they increased to 44 and 56 respectively.

3. R. K. Karanjia, *China Stands Up;* and *Wolves of the Wild Forest,* p. 76.

4. See V. K. R. V. Rao's address at Delhi published in *Hindustan Times,* November 10, 1951; also Pandit Sunderlal's *China Today,* p. 596.

5. According to official Chinese figures, in 1951 alone 1,200,000 "counterrevolutionaries" were liquidated.

6. See Report on New China in Pandit Sunderlal's *China Today,* pp. 557-58.

7. See article by K. A. Abbas in *Blitz,* December 29, 1951; and Sunderlal, *China Today,* Chapter XI.

8. *The Tribune* (Ambala), December 16, 1951.

9. Frank Moraes, *Report on Mao's China,* pp. 17-18. Moraes, the well-known editor of the *Times of India,* was a member of one of these delegations.

10. Moraes, *Report on Mao's China,* p. 18.

11. Sunderlal, *China Today,* pp. 52-53.

12. *Ibid.*, p. 54.

13. *Ibid.*, pp. 56-57.

14. Chanakya Sen, *Tibet Disappears* (1960), p. 115.

15. See the article on "The Impact of Communist China on Visitors from India" by Margaret Fisher and Joan V. Bondurant in *The Far Eastern Review,* February, 1956, pp. 257 ff.

16. *Times of India,* November 9, 1951.

17. These will be found particularly in *Report on Mao's China* by

Frank Moraes, *Window on China* by Raja Hutheesing, and *From My China Diary*, by Braja Kishore Shastri.

18. Fisher and Bondurant, *Indian Views on Sino-Indian Relations*, p. 14. Commenting on this outburst of anti-Indian feeling in China, Mr. Krishna Menon stated: "They appear to be angry with us, but we must not be angry with them." One wishes Mr. Menon had exercised the same restraint and moderation on other similar occasions.

19. Lowell Thomas, *The Silent War in Tibet*, p. 213; also Fisher and Bondurant, *loc. cit.*, pp. 21-23.

20. For the text of the agreement see Chanakya Sen, *Tibet Disappears*, pp. 82-85.

21. Nehru himself was not unaware of the limitations of *Panch Shila* as a panacea for international ills. In his circular on foreign policy addressed to the Congress Party's state units, he said: "It is said, how can you put faith in such declarations? In international affairs, one can never be dead certain and the friends of today might be enemies of tomorrow. That may be so. Are we then to begin with enmity and suspicion and not give any other approach a chance? Surely it is better, with nations as with individuals, to hope for and expect the best, but at the same time to be prepared for any eventuality." (*Congress Bulletin*, No. 5, June-July, 1954, quoted by Fisher and Bondurant, *loc. cit.*, pp. 26-27).

22. Quoted from Prime Minister Nehru's speech in the Lok Sabha, May 18, 1954.

23. It is stated that Sir Girija Shankar Bajpai, then Secretary-General in the Ministry of External Affairs, advised the government of India that the reopening of the Indian consulate at Kashgar should be made an essential condition for the signing of the agreement. His advice was not accepted.

Chapter 5   Hindi Chini Bhai Bhai

1. See *People's China*, February 4, 1950.

2. Quoted from Chou En-lai's address to the members of the Indian Parliament on November 29, 1956, *The Hindu*, December 1, 1956, 9:1.

3. *Keesing's Contemporary Archives*, 1954, p. 13890.

4. *The Hindu*, December 1, 1956, 9:1.

5. *Asian Recorder*, 1956, pp. 1182-85.

6. *Current Background*, No. 439, March 8, 1957.

7. *Asian Recorder*, 1955, p. 139.

8. *The Statesman*, Calcutta, September 8, 1958.

9. Cf. the joint statement issued by Nehru and Tito from Brioni (July 6, 1955), Nehru's statement to newspaper correspondents in Sweden (June 24, 1957), etc.

10. Indian *White Paper* I (1954-59), p. 49.

11. *Ibid.*, p. 46.

12. *Ibid.*

13. *Ibid.*

14. Speaking in the Lok Sabha on April 22, 1959, Prime Minister Nehru stated: "So far as the Russian maps are concerned, I think they had merely copied them from the Chinese maps without probably going into the matter. When we addressed them they said they would look into the matter. So far as the Chinese maps are concerned, we are still in correspondence. As I have previously said, their answer has been that these are old maps, we are not sure of the exact border and we shall look into it and till then the status quo should continue! Well, that is not a very adequate answer, if I may say so, after so many years."

15. Indian *White Paper* I (1954-59), p. 10.

16. *Ibid.*, p. 11.

17. *Ibid.*, pp. 17-18.

18. *Ibid.*, p. 32.

19. *Ibid.*, p. 22.

20. *Ibid.*, p. 33.

21. The area is at an altitude of 16,000 to 17,000 feet, "treeless, grass-less, without a living thing about," as Prime Minister Nehru once described it.

22. Indian *White Paper* I, p. 26.

23. *Ibid.*, pp. 26-28.

24. *Ibid.*, p. 53.

25. For the text of the treaty see *Kashmir Affairs*, Delhi, November-December, 1959, pp. 43-44. The relevant portion in Persian, translated into English, runs as follows: "It is sworn [by the representatives of Tibet and China] to the Almighty that in no way whatsoever will this pledge be disregarded, neglected or deviated from and however the limits and frontiers of the territory of Ladakh with its adjacent lands had been prescribed [or arranged] from time immemorial will absolutely and essentially not be the subject of our designs and intention. We will carry on the trade in wool, shawl and tea, in accordance with the old customs, via Ladakh year by year; and if the opponents of Shri Raja Sahib Bahadur enter our territory and its surroundings, we will not accommodate the afore-mentioned persons in our territory. We will not diverge the least [a hair's breadth] from the agreement of solidarity, friendship and good neighbourliness, and the prescribed limits and frontiers of Ladakh territory, and the pledge to keep open the trade route for wool, shawl and tea, as we have undertaken in writing."

26. Cf. Nehru's statement in the Rajya Sabha on September 1, 1959.

27. See note given by the Chinese Foreign Office to the Counsellor of India, July 10, 1958. Indian *White Paper*, I, p. 60.

28. Indian *White Paper* I, pp. 63-65.

29. *The Statesman* (Calcutta), March 9, 1959. It is some satisfaction that the government of India did not actually carry out the threat.

Chapter 6   Revolt in Tibet

1. The office of the Panchen Lama was created by the fifth Dalai Lama —the "Great Fifth"—to honor one of his favorite teachers, giving him a new name, Panchen Edreni, and assigning to his keeping Tibet's second largest city, Shigatse, and its monasteries. Since then the Panchen Lama has been second in ecclesiastical importance to the Dalai Lama. But his temporal powers have always been limited and he has no rights of succession to the throne of the Dalai Lama. The Chinese have, however, frequently used the Panchen Lama as a "political foil against the Dalai Lama."

2. *Pacific Affairs*, September, 1959, p. 254.

3. Quoted in *The Question of Tibet*, p. 43.

4. *World Jurists' Report on Genocide and Violation of Human Rights*. The Dalai Lama made a statement to the same effect in his Mussoorie news conference. See also *The Question of Tibet*, pp. 204-207.

5. Quoted in Chanakya Sen, *Tibet Disappears*, p. 413.

6. *Pacific Affairs*, June, 1959, p. 175.

7. *South China Morning Post*, January 24, 1959.

8. George N. Patterson, *Tibet in Revolt*, p. 131.

9. *Ibid.*, p. 127.

10. *Ibid.*, p. 174.

11. *Hindustan Times*, March 7, 1959.

12. *Hindustan Times*, March 24, 1959, 5:1.

13. For a full report see *The Question of Tibet*, pp. 163-70.

14. *The Statesman* (Calcutta), May 5, 1959.

15. *The Hindu*, April 18, 1959, 7:4.

16. This is clear from Nehru's address to the Parliamentary Consultative Committee on foreign affairs on April 10, 1959. See *The Hindu*, April 12, 1959.

17. Indian *White Paper* I, 73-76.

18. *Ibid.*, I, 77-78.

Chapter 7   Chinese Intrusions and Claims

1. *The Hindu*, May 18, 1959.

2. *The Hindu*, April 16, 1959, 1:7.

3. *Hindustan Times*, July 1, 1959, 12:2.

4. *White Paper* I, 79.

5. *White Paper* II, 43.

6. *The Statesman* (Calcutta), August 21, 1959.

7. *White Paper* I, pp. 80-82, 86, 93.

8. *White Paper* I, 80-95; II, 70-123. It may be added that a large number of these "trapped" Indian nationals have been allowed to come

back to India in the second half of 1960, but some are still left, a few languishing in Chinese prisons.

9. *White Paper* I, 38-39.

10. *Ibid.*, p. 41.

11. *Ibid.*, I, 44; II, 3-5.

12. *White Paper* II, 34.

13. *Lok Sabha Debates* (Eighth Session), Second series, Vol. XXXIII, No. 19, August 28, 1959, Col. 4796-4801, 4862-4870.

14. *Hindustan Times*, August 31, 1959.

15. *White Paper* II, 27-33.

16. *White Paper* I, 53.

17. *Ibid.*, II, 45.

18. *Ibid.*, II, 34-52.

19. *Hindustan Times*, September 11, 13, 1959.

20. *Ibid.*

21. *White Paper* II, 45.

22. *Hindustan Times*, September 13, 1959.

23. *Hindustan Times*, September 17, 1959.

24. *Hindustan Times*, September 25, 1959.

25. *White Paper* II, 65; *Hindustan Times*, September 26, 1959.

26. *Hindustan Times*, September 27, 1959, 12:5; *Ibid.*, September 3, 1959, 8:7; *White Paper* II, 65-69.

27. *Hindustan Times*, October 19, 1959, 14:5.

28. *Hindustan Times*, October 23, 1959, 10:4.

29. *White Paper* II, 13-26; III, 1-22.

Chapter 8   Delhi Summit

1. *Hindustan Times*, October 29, 1959, 1:2.

2. *Ibid.*, October 31, 1959, 1, 16; November 2, 10:6, 7.

3. *White Paper* III, 46.

4. *Ibid.*, III, 45-46.

5. *White Paper* III, 56.

6. *White Paper* III, 58.

7. *White Paper* III, 60-82.

8. A few days later the Soviet Premier, Mr. Nikita Khrushchev, followed them.

9. *White Paper* III, 99.

10. *Hindustan Times*, April 27, 1960.

Chapter 9   Chinese Claims Examined

1. See Chapter 5 above.

2. *White Paper* I, 16.

3. *White Paper* IV, 14.

4. *Ibid.*, III, 64.

5. *United Asia*, Vol. XII, No. 4, p. 321.

6. *Amrita Bazar Patrika* (Calcutta), February 18, 1960.

7. *White Paper* II, 40.

8. *White Paper* II, 27.

9. *White Paper* III, 72-73.

10. *Ibid.*, III, 73.

11. *Ibid.*, III, 63. The Indian officials who met their Chinese counterparts to discuss the border question have noted how they were "most surprised at the statement of the Chinese side that they distinguished between the actions of past Chinese Governments, accepted what suited them and rejected what was not in consonance with the present Chinese attitude and claims" (*Report of the Officials of the Governments of India and the People's Republic of China on the Boundary Question*, p. 250).

Chapter 10   Retrospect and Prospect

1. A. Doak Barnett, *Communist China and Asia*, p. 66.

2. *Ibid.*, p. 65.

3. Mao Tse-tung. *Problems of War and Strategy*, p. 15.

4. *Current Background*, No. 534, November 12, 1958; also Barnett, *Communist China in Asia*, pp. 106-107.

5. Quoted in *The Statesman* (Calcutta) June 25, 1960, from the Chinese press.

6. Barnett, *Communist China in Asia*, p. 10.

7. Isaac Deutscher. "Soviet Documents on Russia's Quarrel with China." *The Statesman* (Calcutta), July 4 and 5, 1961.

8. Barnett, *Communist China and Asia*, p. 112.

9. For a more detailed account of the Chinese press comments on India in 1949 and 1950 see Girilal Jain, *Panchsheela and After*, Chapter I.

10. *White Paper* II, 45.

11. *The Commonweal*, April 15, 1960.

12. Quoted in George N. Patterson, *Tibet in Revolt*, p. 27.

SELECTED BIBLIOGRAPHY

DOCUMENTS

Aitchison, Sir C., *Collection of Treaties, Engagements and Sanads Relating to India and Neighbouring Countries* (Calcutta, 5th ed. rev.), Vol. XIV.

Asian Recorder (New Delhi).

The Boundary Question between China and Tibet, a valuable record of the Tripartite Conference between China, Britain, and Tibet held in India, 1913-14 (Peking, 1940).

British and Foreign State Papers, 1948, Part II, Vol. 151. London, H.M. Stationery Office, 1956.

Documents on International Affairs, 1950 and 1954, published by the Royal Institute of International Affairs, London.

Foreign Policy of India: Texts of Documents (Lok Sabha Secretariat, New Delhi, 1958).

Keesing's *Contemporary Archives* (1950-1960).

Parliament of India, *Parliamentary Debates,* Official Reports (1950-1960).

Report of the Officials of the Governments of India and the People's Republic of China on the Boundary Question. Ministry of External Affairs, Government of India (February, 1961).

United Nations, General Assembly, Fifth Session, *Official Records* (General Committee, 73rd meeting).

U.S. Department of State, *Foreign Relations of the United States, 1942* (Washington, 1956).

White Paper No. I. Notes, Memoranda and Letters Exchanged and Agreements Signed between the Governments of India and China, 1954-1959. Ministry of External Affairs, Government of India.

White Paper No. II. Notes, Memoranda and Letters Exchanged between the Governments of India and China, September-November, 1959, and a note on the Historical Background of the Himalayan Frontier. Ministry of External Affairs, Government of India.

White Paper No. III. Notes, Memoranda and Letters Exchanged between the Governments of India and China, November 1959-March, 1960. Ministry of External Affairs, Government of India.

White Paper No. IV. Notes, Memoranda and Letters Exchanged between the Governments of India and China, March, 1960-November, 1960. Ministry of External Affairs, Government of India.

BOOKS

Barnett, A. Doak, *Communist China and Asia* (Harper, New York, 1961).

Bell, Sir Charles, *Tibet Past and Present* (2nd ed., Oxford, 1927).

——, *Portrait of the Dalai Lama* (Oxford, 1946).

Bowles, Chester, *Ambassador's Report* (Harper, New York, 1954).

Brecher, Michael, *Nehru—A Political Biography* (Oxford, 1959).

——, *Indian Foreign Policy: An Interpretation* (New York, 1957).

Chandrasekhar, S., *A Decade of Mao's China* (Perennial Press, Bombay, 1960).

——, *Communist China Today* (Asia Publishing House, Bombay, 1961).

Collective Defence in South East Asia: The Manila Treaty and Its Implications, Royal Institute of International Affairs (London, 1956).

Economic Development of India and Communist China, U.S. Senate Committee on Foreign Relations, Sub-Committee on Technical

Assistance Programs, Staff Study No. 6, 84th Congress, 2nd Sess. (Washington, D.C., Government Printing Office, 1956).

Fifield, Russell H., *The Diplomacy of Southeast Asia*, 1945-1958 (Harper, New York, 1958).

Fisher, Margaret Welpley and Bondurant, Joan Valérie, *Indian Views on Sino-Indian Relations*, Indian Press Digests—Monograph Series, No. I, 1956. (Institute of International Studies, University of California, Berkeley, California.)

Gluckstein, Ygael, *Mao's China: Economic and Political Survey* (Boston, Beacon Press, 1957).

Guillain, Robert, *600 Million Chinese* (Criterion Books, New York, 1957).

Hutheesing, Raja, *Window on China* (London, 1953).

——, *The Great Peace: An Asian's Candid Report on Red China* (Harper, New York, 1953).

Indian Year Book of International Affairs (Madras), 1954.

Jain, Girilal, *Panchsheela and After* (Asia Publishing House, Bombay, 1960).

Karanjia, K.R., *China Stands Up* and *Wolves of the Wild Forest* (People's Publishing House, Bombay, 1952).

Karunakaran Nayar, Vellamkulath, *India in World Affairs*, Vols. I and II (Oxford University Press, 1952 and 1958).

Levi, Werner, *Free India in Asia* (University of Minnesota Press, 1953).

——, *Modern China's Foreign Policy* (University of Minnesota Press, 1953).

Li Tieh-tseng, *The Historical Status of Tibet* (Columbia University Press, 1956).

Mao Tse-tung, *Problems of War and Strategy* (Foreign Languages Press, Peking, 1954).

——, *Selected Works* (Lawrence and Wishart Ltd., London, 1954).

Menon, K.P.S., *Delhi—Chungking, A Travel Diary* (Oxford, 1947).

Moraes, Frank, *Report on Mao's China* (Macmillan, New York, 1953).

——, *The Revolt in Tibet* (Macmillan, New York, 1960).

Panikkar, K.M., *In Two Chinas* (3rd ed., George Allen and Unwin, London, 1955).

Patterson, George N. *Tibet in Revolt* (Faber and Faber, London, 1960).

Petech, L., *China and Tibet in the Early Eighteenth Century* (Leyden, 1950).

The Question of Tibet and the Rule of Law, published by the International Commission of Jurists, Geneva, 1959.

Radhakrishnan, Sir Sarvapalli, *India and China* (2nd ed., Hind Kitab Ltd., Bombay, 1947).

Richardson, Hugh, *Red Star over Tibet* (Delhi, 1959).

Rockhill, W.W., *Dalai Lamas of Lhasa and Their Relations with the Manchu Emperors of China* (1644-1908).

Sen, Chanakya, *Tibet Disappears* (Asia Publishing House, Bombay, 1960).

Shastri, Braja Kishore, *From My China Diary* (Delhi, Siddartha Publications).

Sitaramayya, B. Pattabhi, *History of the Indian National Congress*, 2 vols. (Padma Publications Ltd., Bombay, 1946-47).

Snow, Edgar, *Red Star Over China* (Random House, New York, 1938), revised edition.

Sundarlal, Pandit, *China Today* (Hindustan Culture Society, Allahabad, 1952).

Talbot, Phillips, and Poplai, Sundarlal, *India and America: A Study in Their Relations* (Harper, New York, 1958).

Tang, Peter S.H., *Communist China Today: Domestic and Foreign Policies* (Praeger, New York, 1957).

Teichman, Erich, *Travels in Eastern Tibet* (Cambridge University Press, 1922).

Thomas, Lowell, *The Silent War in Tibet* (New York, 1959).

Tibet and the Chinese People's Republic: A Report to the International Commission of Jurists by its Legal Enquiry Committee on Tibet (Geneva, International Commission of Jurists, 1960).

Waddell, L.A., *Lhasa and Its Mysteries* (Methuen and Co., London, 1905).

Walker, Richard L., *China under Communism: The First Five Years* (Yale University Press, 1955).

World Jurists' Report on Genocide and Violation of Human Rights, Geneva, June 5, 1960.

Younghusband, Sir Francis, *India and Tibet* (London, 1910).

MAGAZINES

American Economic Review.
Annals of the American Academy of Political and Social Science.
The China Quarterly, (London).
China Reconstructs (Peking).
The Communist (Bombay).
Current History (Philadelphia, Pennsylvania).
Eastern Economist (Bombay).
Far Eastern Survey (New York).
Foreign Affairs: An American Quarterly Review.
India Quarterly (Indian Council of World Affairs, New Delhi).
Modern Review (Calcutta).
The Nation, (New York).
Pacific Affairs (New York).
Peking Review (Peking).
Round Table (London).
United Asia (Bombay).
World Culture (Shanghai).
World Politics (Princeton, New Jersey).

NEWSPAPERS

Amrita Bazar Patrika (Calcutta).
The Hindu (Madras).
The Hindu Weekly (Madras).
Hindustan Standard (Calcutta and Delhi).
Hindustan Times (Delhi).
The Overseas Hindustan Times (Delhi).
The Statesman (Calcutta and Delhi).
The Times of India (Bombay and Delhi).
The Tribune (Ambala).

INDEX

Note: For treaties, conventions, and agreements *see* treaties; for conferences *see* conferences.